Cooking Collections

Canadian Feasts From Land And Sea

By
Federated Women's Institutes of Canada

Front Cover — Cranberry Pork Chops, page 30; Chinese Asparagus, page 74; Gourmet Wild Rice and Cheese Casserole, page 121; Peach Pie, page 106.

Cooking Collections
By Federated Women's Institutes of Canada

Compiled and coordinated by
Jennie McInnes
Edited by
Mary Elizabeth Stewart

Second Printing — March 1990

Canadian Cataloguing in Publication Data
Main entry under title:

Cooking collections : Canadian feasts from land and sea

  Coordinator: Jennie McInnes.
  Includes index.
  ISBN 0-919845-65-7

1. Cookery, Canadian. I. Federated Women's
Institutes of Canada. II. McInnes, Jennie, 1933-
TX715.C66   1988   641.5971   C88-098095-8

Photography by
Patricia Holdsworth
Patricia Holdsworth Photography
Regina, Saskatchewan

Dishes and Accessories Compliments of
Junors The Kitchen Collection, Regina, Saskatchewan

Designed, Printed and Produced in Canada by
Centax Books, a Division of M·C·Graphics Inc.

Publishing Consultant and Food Stylist: Margo Embury
Design by Blair Fraser
1048 Fleury Street
Regina, Saskatchewan, Canada S4N 4W8
(306) 359-3737   Fax (306) 525-3955

𝔉𝔢𝔡𝔢𝔯𝔞𝔱𝔢𝔡 𝔚𝔬𝔪𝔢𝔫'𝔰 𝔍𝔫𝔰𝔱𝔦𝔱𝔲𝔱𝔢𝔰 𝔬𝔣 ℭ𝔞𝔫𝔞𝔡𝔞

CONSTITUENT SOCIETY, ASSOCIATED COUNTRY WOMEN OF THE WORLD

National Office
Suite 606, 251 Bank St.
Ottawa, Ont. K2P 1X3
(613) 234-1090

On behalf of the Federated Women's Institutes of Canada I am pleased to introduce you to "Cooking Collections of the Federated Women's Institute of Canada."

The recipes in this book have been contributed by Women's Institute Members in all ten Provinces of Canada. In addition, well-known Canadians have shared their culinary specialties with us.

We have endeavored to acquaint you with the products grown and harvested across Canada. As you look through the pages, recipes and pictures bring the culinary art and traditions of Canada alive. Yes, our country is rich and abundant in the products of the land and the sea.

We are especially proud of the wonderful spirit of cooperation of Canadians who have made "Cooking Collections" possible.

Beatrice Reeves

President,
Federated Women's Institutes of Canada

Cooking Collections
of
The Federated Women's Institutes
of Canada

Compiled and Coordinated by JENNIE MCINNES
Edited by MARY ELIZABETH STEWART

Introduction

The committee wishes to acknowledge the generous assistance of the Provincial Offices for their enthusiastic support by submitting recipes, pictures, and other material for this national cookbook.

This cookbook reflects the varied life styles and eating habits of our country from the early years to modern times.

Jennie McInnes N.S.W.I.
June Bell B.C.W.I.

Table of Contents

Food measurements in this cookbook are given in both U.S. standard and metric. Recipes have been tested in standard and the rounded metric equivalents are given as a convenience for those who are more familiar with metric.

Metric Cooking

The recipes collected for this cookbook have been tested by W.I. members in the U.S. Standard System. They have been converted to the Metric System but may require slight adjustments, as such conversions are not always exact.

Basic Metric Measures:

Length	— centimeter (cm)
Volume	— milliliter (mL)
	— liter (L)
Weight	— gram (g)
	— kilogram (kg)
Temperature	— degree Celsius (°C)

Metric Equivalents:

Volume:

U.S. Standard	Metric
¼ tsp.	1 mL
½ tsp.	2 mL
¾ tsp.	3 mL
1 tsp.	5 mL
1 tbsp.	15 mL
2 tbsp.	25 mL
¼ cup	50 mL
⅓ cup	75 mL
½ cup	125 mL
⅔ cup	150 mL
¾ cup	175 mL
1 cup	250 mL
4 cups	1000 mL (1 L)

Weight:

U.S. Standard	Metric
¼ lb.	125 g
½ lb.	250 g
¾ lb.	375 g
1 lb.	500 g
2 lbs.	1 kg

Temperature:

150°F	= 70°C
200°F	= 100°C
250°F	= 120°C
300°F	= 150°C
325°F	= 160°C
350°F	= 180°C
375°F	= 190°C
400°F	= 200°C
425°F	= 220°C
450°F	= 230°C

Utensils:

Baking Dish	8" square	= 2 L
	9" square	= 2.5 L
	12 x 8"	= 3 L
	13 x 9"	= 4 L
	14 x 10"	= 5 L
Loaf Pan	8 x 4"	= 1.5 L
	9 x 5"	= 2 L
	10 x 5"	= 3 L
Pie Plate	9"	= 23 cm (1 L)

Newfoundland

Famous For Fish

We begin our collection of Canadian recipes on the East Coast — in the province of Newfoundland. It would be impossible to talk about food and Newfoundland in the same sentence and not think "fish". The history of Newfoundland is interwoven with the development of the fisheries to such an extent that superstitions, customs and omens of good or bad luck related to the fisheries are well known throughout the province. Read on to discover some of the "fisheries folklore" of Newfoundland.

— If small fish come in first, the fishermen say it is a sign of a good fishery.
— In many places it is a common belief among fishermen that unless the boat is turned from the sun from the east to the west, they will have no luck.
— It is considered unlucky to count your fish while fishing.
— Much snow in winter is thought to foretell a good fishery for the spring and summer.
— If a codfish is heavier to haul up than usual, a windstorm is approaching.
— A charm for a toothache is to take out the finbone of a haddock, when the fish is yet alive, and wear the bone around the neck in a bag.
—The first fish caught for the season should be eaten by the fisherman, else he will not have a good season.
— For the alleviation of rheumatic pains, fishermen often carry a haddock's bone in their pocket.
— If a fish remains forgotten in the boat, when the others are taken out, it is a sign of bad luck for the catcher. Such a fish is called a "witch" and some fishermen making the discovery would not fish on that day.

Though Newfoundland is famous for fish, many other delicious recipes also originate in this province. We present, for your enjoyment, two traditional Newfoundland Christmas recipes, followed by a collection of fish recipes. Remember, in Newfoundland "fish" means "cod"; other species are specifically mentioned by name!

8

Baked Cod Fillets with Shrimp Sauce, page 12

Figgy Duff with Molasses Coady

2 cups	dry bread crusts	500 mL
	water	
1 cup	seedless raisins	250 mL
½ cup	molasses	125 mL
¼ cup	melted butter	50 mL
1 tsp.	baking soda	5 mL
1 tbsp.	hot water	15 mL
½ cup	flour	125 mL
1 tsp.	ground ginger	5 mL
1 tsp.	allspice	5 mL
1 tsp.	cinnamon	5 mL
½ tsp.	salt	2 mL
	Molasses Coady	

Soak bread crusts in small amount of water until soft. Remove and drain, squeezing gently. Break into crumbs and measure out 2 cups (500 mL). Combine crumbs, raisins, molasses and melted butter. Mix baking soda in hot water, then stir into crumb mixture. Combine flour, ginger, allspice, cinnamon and salt. Add to crumb mixture and stir until mixed. Pour into a greased pudding mold; fill about ⅔ full. Cover with foil or a heavy teacloth. Place mold on a trivet in a heavy kettle over 1-2" (2.5-5 cm) of boiling water. Cover kettle and steam for 2 hours, use high heat at first then turn heat down to medium-low. Serve hot topped with Molasses Coady (see recipe below).

Molasses Coady

1 cup	molasses	250 mL
¼ cup	water	50 mL
¼ cup	butter	50 mL
1 tbsp.	vinegar	15 mL

Combine ingredients in a saucepan. Boil for 10 minutes, stirring to mix. Serve hot over Figgy Duff (see recipe above). **Yield:** 1 cup (250 mL).

Old-Fashioned Christmas Pork Cake

1 cup	finely ground salt pork	250 mL
1 cup	hot strong coffee	250 mL
1 cup	sugar	250 mL
1 tsp.	allspice	5 mL
1 tsp.	nutmeg	5 mL
1 tsp.	cinnamon	5 mL
1 tsp.	baking soda	5 mL
2	eggs, well beaten	2
⅔ cup	molasses	150 mL
3 cups	flour	750 mL
2 cups	raisins	500 mL
1 cup	currants	250 mL
2 cups	mixed peel	500 mL

Place pork in a bowl, pour hot coffee over it and let stand until cold. Combine sugar, spices and baking soda. Stir this into pork mixture and then add eggs and molasses. Add all but 2 tbsp. (25 mL) flour to pork mixture. Mix well. Sprinkle 2 tbsp. (25 mL) flour over fruit and stir into batter. Line a 9" or 10" (2.5 L) baking dish with several layers of brown paper and turn batter into the dish. Bake at 275°F (140°C) for about 3 hours.

Gourmet Caplin
(Newfie Springtime)

1 lb.	fresh caplin	500 g
¼ cup	melted butter	50 mL
1	garlic clove, minced	1
¼ cup	fine bread crumbs	50 mL
¼ cup	grated Parmesan cheese	50 mL
2 tbsp.	chopped parsley	25 mL
	salt and pepper to taste	

Clean caplin and pat dry with paper towel. Add garlic to melted butter. Combine crumbs, cheese, parsley, salt and pepper. Dip fish in garlic butter, then roll in crumbs. Put in a single layer in a large, shallow baking dish. Bake at 450°F (230°C) for 8 minutes or until brown and fish flakes easily with a fork.
Serves: 4.

Banquet Baked Fish

1	whole fish (cod OR salmon), cleaned and dressed	1

Stuffing:

3 tbsp.	butter	50 mL
1	onion, finely diced	1
3 cups	bread crumbs	750 mL
½ cup	water	125 mL
¼ tsp.	sage	1 mL
½ tsp.	salt	2 mL
1 tsp.	savory	5 mL
dash	pepper	dash
¼ lb.	mild cheese, grated OR finely diced	125 g

Seasoned Flour:

3 tbsp.	flour	50 mL
½ tsp.	savory	2 mL
¼ tsp.	sage	1 mL
¼ tsp.	salt	1 mL
dash	pepper	dash
¾ cup	hot water	175 mL

Gravy:

4 tbsp.	butter	60 mL
¼ cup	flour	50 mL
3 tbsp.	lemon juice	50 mL
3 tbsp.	sugar	50 mL
1½ cups	water	375 mL

Prepare stuffing by sautéing onion in butter. Add onion to bread crumbs along with water, sage, salt, savory, pepper and ½ the cheese. Reserve remaining cheese for gravy. Pack stuffing firmly inside fish. Prepare seasoned flour by mixing the flour with the savory, sage, salt and pepper. Dredge whole fish in seasoned flour and place in baking dish with hot water. Bake at 350°F (180°C) for about 50 minutes or until browned and tender, basting frequently. Prepare gravy while fish is baking. Cream butter with flour. Add lemon juice, sugar and water. Cook over low heat, stirring in reserved cheese. Add to gravy in baking dish. Baste fish again with thickened gravy. **Serving Suggestion:** Serve on a platter and garnish with lettuce, sliced lemon and tomato. **Serves:** 4-6.

Golden Fish Bake

2 lbs.	frozen fish fillets	1 kg
¼ cup	flour	50 mL
1 tsp.	salt	5 mL
dash	pepper	dash
1 cup	milk	250 mL
2 cups	soft bread crumbs	500 mL
¼ cup	butter	50 mL
1 tsp.	dill seed	5 mL
1 cup	sour cream	250 mL
1	lemon, sliced	1
	parsley sprigs	

Cut frozen fillets in serving-size portions. Coat with flour and sprinkle with salt and pepper. Arrange in a single layer in a greased baking dish. Pour milk over fish. Bake, uncovered, at 425°F (220°C) for 20 minutes. Toast crumbs lightly in butter in a frying pan. Stir dill seed into sour cream. Remove fish from the oven and spread with cream mixture. Top with toasted crumbs and bake an additional 5 minutes or until cream mixture is set. Garnish with lemon slices and parsley sprigs. **Serves:** 6-8.

Baked Cod Fillets with Shrimp Sauce

1 lb.	fresh frozen cod fillets	500 g
3 tbsp.	butter	50 mL
3 tbsp.	flour	50 mL
1 cup	hot water	250 mL
2 tsp.	lemon juice	10 mL
4 oz.	can, cocktail shrimp, including liquid	113 g
	paprika	

Thaw cod fillets and place in a greased baking dish in a single layer. Melt butter and blend in flour. Stir in hot water and lemon juice and cook until thick. Stir in shrimp and liquid. Pour sauce over cod fillets and sprinkle with paprika. Bake at 325°F (160°C) for about 15 minutes or until cod flakes. Serve at once. **Serves:** 4. See photograph on page 8A.

Cod au Gratin

4 tbsp.	butter	60 mL
2 tsp.	flour	10 mL
1 tsp.	salt	5 mL
½ tsp.	pepper	2 mL
2 cups	milk	500 mL
2½ cups	cooked, flaked, cooled, fresh codfish	625 mL
1 cup	grated cheese	250 mL

Melt butter, add flour, salt and pepper. Stir to form a paste. Add milk slowly, stirring to blend. Cook until thick, stirring frequently. Grease a 2-quart (2 L) baking dish and pour a little of the sauce in the bottom. Add a layer of cod. Sprinkle on ⅓ of the cheese. Repeat layers, finishing with remaining sauce topped with last ⅓ of cheese. Bake at 350°F (180°C) for about 30 minutes. **Serves:** 4.

Fillet Bubbly Bake

1 lb.	frozen fillets	500 g
10 oz.	can, cream of mushroom soup	284 mL
¼ cup	chopped onion	50 mL
1 tbsp.	lemon juice	15 mL
½ cup	grated cheese	125 mL

Cut fillets in 4 portions and place in a single layer in a shallow, greased baking dish. Combine the soup, onion and lemon juice, then pour over the fillets. Top with cheese. Bake at 450°F (230°C) for 20 minutes. **Serves:** 4.

Sweet and Sour Cod

2 lbs.	cod fillets	1 kg
	butter	
¾ cup	chopped celery	175 mL
¾ cup	chopped onion	175 mL
¼ cup	vinegar	50 mL
¼ cup	white sugar	50 mL
¼ cup	flour	50 mL
2 cups	water	500 mL
dash	salt	dash
	chives, chopped (optional)	

Fry cod lightly in butter, then remove and place in a single layer in a greased baking dish. Sauté celery and onion adding more butter to the frying pan, if necessary. Mix together vinegar, sugar, flour, water, salt and chives. Stir in sautéed celery and onion and pour over fish. Bake at 350°F (180°C) for 10 minutes. **Serves:** 4-6.

Barbecued Fish

1½ lbs.	fish fillets	750 g
1	medium onion, diced	1
1 tbsp.	butter	15 mL
¾ cup	ketchup	175 mL
¼ cup	vinegar	50 mL
2 tbsp.	brown sugar	25 mL
	salt and pepper to taste	

Place fish in a single layer in a greased baking dish. In a frying pan, lightly sauté onion in butter. Add remaining ingredients. Simmer for 5 minutes. Pour sauce over fish. Bake at 350°F (180°C) for 30 minutes. **Serving Suggestion:** Serve with creamed potatoes and green peas or string beans. **Serves:** 4-6.

Fish Cakes

2 cups	mashed potatoes	500 mL
1	egg, well beaten	1
1 lb.	salt cod	500 g
½ tsp.	onion juice	2 mL
	flour	
	melted butter	

Combine potatoes, egg, salt cod and onion juice. Mix well, then form into patties. Roll in flour and fry in melted butter until light golden brown on both sides. **Serving Suggestion:** Serve with tomato sauce. **Serves:** 4.

Fish Quiche

1	9" (23 cm) unbaked pastry shell	1
1 tbsp.	butter	15 mL
¼ cup	chopped onion	50 mL
4	eggs	4
1¼ cups	milk	300 mL
pinch	nutmeg	pinch
¼ tsp.	Tabasco sauce	1 mL
pinch	salt	pinch
1 cup	cooked salmon, tuna, mackerel OR cod	250 mL
1 cup	grated cheese	250 mL

Chill pastry, then bake at 450°F (230°C) for 5 minutes. Meanwhile, sauté onion in butter. Beat the eggs and add milk and spices. Line the bottom of the pastry shell with the fish and sautéed onion. Pour the egg mixture over the fish. Sprinkle with cheese. Bake at 350°F (180°C) for 25-30 minutes until browned and filling is set. **Serving Suggestion:** Delicious served with tossed salad and warm rolls. **Serves:** 6.

Fish Chowder

2 tbsp.	chopped salt pork	25 mL
1	medium onion, chopped	1
2 cups	diced potatoes	500 mL
½ cup	sliced carrots	125 mL
1 tsp.	salt	5 mL
dash	pepper	dash
2 cups	boiling water	500 mL
1 lb.	fish fillets	500 g
2 cups	milk	500 mL

Fry salt pork, then drain off fat. Add onions and sauté until light brown. Place pork-onion mixture into a large saucepan and add vegetables, salt, pepper and water. Simmer until tender. Cut fish in serving-size pieces and add to vegetables. Boil for 10 minutes. Add milk and simmer, but do NOT boil. **Serves:** 4-6.

Perky Salt Cod Chowder

1 lb.	salt cod, soaked, drained, cooked and flaked*	500 g
2 tbsp.	butter	25 mL
½ cup	chopped onion	125 mL
½ cup	diced celery	125 mL
⅓ cup	diced green pepper	75 mL
3½ cups	water	875 mL
19 oz.	can, tomatoes	540 mL
19 oz.	can, tomato juice	540 mL
¾ cup	ketchup	175 mL
¼ cup	uncooked instant rice	50 mL
2 tbsp.	pickling spice	25 mL
2	garlic cloves, quartered	2
½ tsp.	paprika	2 mL
2-4 drops	Tabasco sauce	2-4 drops
1 tsp.	Worcestershire sauce	5 mL

Prepare cod and set aside. In a large saucepan, melt the butter. Add onion, celery and green pepper. Sauté until tender. Add water, tomatoes, tomato juice, ketchup and rice. Tie pickling spice and garlic in a spice bag and add to the saucepan. Simmer for 30 minutes. Add paprika, Tabasco sauce, Worcestershire sauce and prepared fish. Reheat. Remove spice bag before serving.

*Note: Using a glass, enamel or stainless steel dish, soak salt cod in water for up to 48 hours. Change water several times. Drain. Place cod in cold water or fish stock and simmer for 20-30 minutes. Drain, skin, bone and flake cod. Yield of 1 lb. (500 g) of dried cod is equal to about 2 cups (500 mL) flaked fish. **Serves:** 12.

Broiled Halibut Steak

2 lbs.	halibut steaks, 1" (2.5 cm) thick	1 kg
½ cup	soy sauce	125 mL
¼ cup	ketchup	50 mL
¼ cup	chopped parsley	50 mL
½ cup	orange juice	125 mL
2	garlic cloves, minced	2
2 tbsp.	lemon juice	25 mL
1 tsp.	pepper	5 mL

Cut steaks into serving-size pieces. Combine remaining ingredients, mixing well. Pour over fish and let marinate for 1 hour. Place fish in a greased, hinged, wire grill about 4" (10 cm) from hot coals. Cook about 8-10 minutes on each side, or until fish flakes easily. Baste frequently with marinade during barbecuing. **Serves:** 4-6.

Halibut Steak Hash

2½ cups	flaked, steamed fresh OR frozen halibut, about 1½ lbs. (750 g) raw	625 mL
3 cups	peeled, boiled, chopped potatoes	750 mL
	salt and pepper to taste	
	bacon fat OR salt pork drippings	

Combine fish and potatoes and season with salt and pepper Heat enough fat or drippings to cover bottom of frying pan. Add fish mixture and stir until heated through. Cook slowly until well browned on bottom. Serve with ketchup or chili sauce. **Serves:** 4.

Salmon Coquilles

	buttered pastry shells	
1	large tomato, peeled and chopped	1
¼ cup	butter	50 mL
2 tbsp.	flour	25 mL
½ cup	chopped canned mushrooms, reserving ½ cup (125 mL) liquid*	125 mL
1 tbsp.	lemon juice	15 mL
1 tbsp.	sherry	15 mL
1 tbsp.	milk	15 mL
2 cups	coarsely flaked salmon	500 mL
1 tsp.	minced onion	5 mL
	salt and pepper to taste	
1½ tsp.	sugar	7 mL
1 cup	buttered bread crumbs	250 mL

Prepare pastry shells. Sauté tomato in butter in a frying pan. Remove tomato. Add flour to liquid in pan and blend. Stir in reserved mushroom liquid, lemon juice, sherry and milk. Cook until thick, stirring thoroughly. Add mushrooms, tomato, salmon, onion, salt, pepper and sugar. Mix well. Spoon into buttered pastry shells. Sprinkle with buttered bread crumbs. Bake at 350°F (180°C) for 20 minutes. **Note:** Fresh mushrooms may be used and milk substituted for the mushroom liquid.

Grilled Salmon Steaks

2 lbs.	salmon steaks, 1" (2.5 cm) thick	1 kg
3 tbsp.	lemon juice	50 mL
1 tsp.	grated lemon peel	5 mL
¼ cup	vegetable oil	50 mL
½ tsp.	salt	2 mL
dash	pepper	dash
¼ tsp.	marjoram	1 mL
1 tbsp.	finely chopped onion	15 mL

Place fish in a single layer in a shallow pan. Combine remaining ingredients and pour over fish. Marinate fish for 30 minutes, turning once. Place fish in a greased, hinged wire grill about 4" (10 cm) from hot coals. Cook 8-10 minutes on each side or until fish flakes easily when tested with a fork. **Serves:** 4-6.

Salmon Loaf

2½ cups	cooked salmon OR 1 lb. (500 g) can, undrained	625 mL
1	egg, beaten	1
⅔ cup	bread crumbs	150 mL
⅔ cup	milk	150 mL
2 tbsp.	melted butter	25 mL
1 tsp.	salt	5 mL

Remove bones from salmon. Add all remaining ingredients and mix well. Put in a greased loaf pan. Bake at 350°F (180°C) for 25-30 minutes. Turn out onto a platter. **Serving Suggestion:** Serve with a medium white sauce to which a chopped hard-cooked egg has been added. **Serves:** 4.

Flipper Pie

	pastry for a single crust	
	seal flippers	
	cold water	
1 tbsp.	baking soda	15 mL
	flour, seasoned with salt	
	rendered pork fat	
	onion and other vegetables of your choice, cut as for stew, potatoes cooked separately OR along with other vegetables	
	salt and pepper to taste	
1 cup	water	250 mL

Prepare pastry. Soak flippers in cold water to which the baking soda has been added. The fat will turn white. Remove all fat as it has a very disagreeable flavor and will ruin the taste of the pie. Dredge flippers in flour seasoned with salt and fry until brown in pork fat. Add a little water and simmer until tender. Place cooked flippers in a roaster along with onion and other desired vegetables, potatoes, seasoning and water. When vegetables are cooked, top with pastry and bake at 425°F (220°C) until nicely browned, about 15-20 minutes.
Serves: 6-8.

Baked Squid

1	squid	1
	bread stuffing	
	fat back pork	

Remove head, insides and tail from squid. Peel off reddish skin, pull out bone and, turning the cone-shaped body inside out, remove fat. Wash well and boil for about 50 minutes. Drain. When cool, stuff with a bread stuffing. Bake at 350°F (180°C) with a little fat back pork for 1½ hours.

Curried Squid Chow Mein

8-10	skinned squid, cut into strips	8-10
	salt and pepper to taste	
	curry powder to taste	
2 cups	chicken bouillon	500 mL
3	celery stalks, sliced	3
2	medium carrots, sliced	2
2	medium onions, quartered	2
1 cup	cauliflower florets and/OR broccoli	250 mL
¼	head cabbage, sliced	¼
½	green pepper, diced	½
1 cup	sliced mushrooms	250 mL
2 tbsp.	cornstarch, dissolved in cold water	25 mL

Fry squid until brown. Season with salt, pepper and curry powder to taste. Add bouillon and simmer slowly for about 1 hour. Add celery, carrots, onion, cauliflower, broccoli and cabbage and cook for another 15 minutes. Add the green pepper and mushrooms during the last 5 minutes of cooking. Make a smooth paste using the cornstarch and a little cold water. Add to the pan, stir and heat the mixture until thickened. **Serves:** 4-6.

Nova Scotia

The Berry Best

Many Nova Scotians will agree that their very best recipes are also their "berry best"! Nova Scotia is blessed with an abundance of berries, most varieties having grown here for centuries. Early settlers to the province were quick to see the benefits of berries — foods that had been used by Native people not only as food, but also for a variety of other practical and medicinal purposes. The long history of the berry has led to some unique uses over the years. Can you imagine using some of these home remedies today?

— To remove freckles, crush some strawberries and rub them on the face before going to bed.
— Teaberries and molasses make a good cough medicine.
— To cure a cold, take 2 tbsp. (25 mL) of black currant jam and crush it in a large cup until all the juice comes out. Add 2 tsp. (10 mL) sugar and fill the cup with boiling water. Drink black currant "tea" as you sit with your feet in a pan of hot water, into which 1 tsp. (5 mL) of dry mustard has been stirred. Go to bed and keep warm for an hour or two.
— Diarrhoea was thought to be cured by drinking Blackberry Cordial. This was made by combining 2 quarts (2 L) juice, 1 lb. (500 g) sugar, and ½ oz. (15 g) cloves (pulverized). This was boiled for a short while and when cooled, a pint (500 mL) of brandy was added.
— Tea made from strawberry leaves was also often used as a remedy for diarrhoea.
— Gooseberry thorns were often used by Native people as probes for boils, for removing splinters and for tattooing.

As you can see, the berry has had an interesting history. Today, Nova Scotians enjoy the many local varieties, including blueberries, blackberries, cranberries, strawberries and many others, in a host of delicious recipes. After trying the following two traditional Nova Scotia recipes, move on to the collection of the "berry best"!

Solomon Gundy

2	salt herring	2
	cold water	
1 cup	vinegar	250 mL
1 tbsp.	sugar	15 mL
dash	pepper	dash
1	large onion, sliced	1

Clean the herring thoroughly; remove skin, fillet and cut in 2" (5 cm) pieces. Soak in cold water for 5 hours, changing the water frequently, or soak overnight if desired. Drain. Heat vinegar and add sugar and pepper. Cool. Pack herring pieces and onion slices in sterilized jars and pour vinegar over to cover. Seal and refrigerate. Let stand 1-2 days before using. **Serving Suggestion:** Makes a great appetizer served on crackers or buttered bread squares.

Apple Dumplings Acadien

Dumplings:

2 cups	flour	500 mL
4 tsp.	baking powder	20 mL
1 tsp.	salt	5 mL
4 tbsp.	shortening	60 mL
¾ cup	milk	175 mL
5-6	apples, pared and thinly sliced	5-6
	sugar	
	cinnamon	
	butter	

Topping:

2 cups	boiling water	500 mL
1 cup	sugar	250 mL
1½ tsp.	butter	7 mL
dash	cinnamon	dash
pinch	nutmeg	pinch

Prepare dumplings by combining the first 3 ingredients. Cut in shortening and add milk to form dough. Roll out like pie crust and cut into 8 squares. Place several apple slices on each square. Top each square with about 2 tsp. (10 mL) sugar, sprinkle with cinnamon and dot with butter. Gather dough around apple slices by pinching corners together. Place in a deep pan or small roaster. Prepare topping by combining all ingredients and pour over dumplings. Bake, covered, at 350°F (180°C) for 45-60 minutes. **Serving Suggestion:** Serve as is, or with cream, whipped cream or ice cream. **Yield:** 8 dumplings.

Apple-Blackberry Pie

	pastry for 2-crust, 9" (23 cm) pie	
2 cups	peeled, chopped apples	500 mL
2 cups	blackberries	500 mL
⅔-¾ cup	sugar	150-175 mL
½ tsp.	nutmeg	2 mL
dash	salt	dash
1 tbsp.	lemon juice	15 mL
1 tbsp.	flour	15 mL
1 tbsp.	butter	15 mL

Line pie plate with half the pastry. Combine all other ingredients, except butter and mix well. Turn into prepared pie shell. Dot with butter. Cover with remaining pastry, seal edges and cut steam vents. Bake in a 375°F (190°C) oven for 45 minutes. **Serves:** 6. See photograph on page 24A.

Blueberry Scones

2 cups	flour	500 mL
¼ cup	sugar	50 mL
3 tsp.	baking powder	15 mL
1 tsp.	salt	5 mL
⅓ cup	butter	75 mL
½ cup	fresh blueberries	125 mL
½ cup	milk	125 mL
2	eggs	2
	sugar	

Combine the dry ingredients. Cut in butter with pastry blender until mixture resembles coarse crumbs. Stir in blueberries. Add milk, 1 whole egg and 1 egg yolk (reserving 1 egg white). Stir with fork until all ingredients are moist. Turn dough out onto a lightly floured surface. Knead quickly and roll out into a circular shape about ½" (1.3 cm) thick. Brush with beaten egg white and sprinkle with sugar. Cut into pie-shaped wedges and place on ungreased baking sheet. Bake at 425°F (220°C) for 12-15 minutes. Serve hot with butter. **Yield:** 12 scones.

Blueberry Ambrosia

1 cup	fresh blueberries	250 mL
1 cup	sliced peaches	250 mL
1 cup	drained, crushed pineapple	250 mL
2 cups	diced marshmallows	500 mL
1 cup	sour cream	250 mL
2 tbsp.	sugar	25 mL

Combine all ingredients together in a bowl. Let stand, refrigerated, for at least 1 hour before serving. Stir occasionally during this time. **Serves:** 6.

Blueberry Squares

Base:

3 tbsp.	butter	50 mL
⅓ cup	sugar	75 mL
2	egg yolks	2
⅔ cup	flour	150 mL
1 tsp.	baking powder	5 mL
1 tsp.	salt	5 mL
¼ cup	milk	50 mL
¼ tsp.	vanilla	1 mL

Topping:

2	egg whites	2
6 tbsp.	sugar	100 mL
¼ tsp.	salt	1 mL
1 cup	fresh OR frozen blueberries, drained	250 mL

Prepare base by creaming butter and sugar together. Add egg yolks, beating well. Combine flour, baking powder and salt, and add to butter mixture alternately with milk and vanilla, beating well after each addition. Pour batter into a well-greased 8" (2 L) square baking dish. Bake at 325-350°F (160-180°C) for 18-20 minutes. Prepare topping by beating egg whites with sugar and salt until well beaten. Fold in blueberries. Spread topping mixture over base. Return to oven and bake for an additional 12-15 minutes or until golden brown. When cooled, cut in squares. **Yield:** 9 squares.

Blueberry Cheesecake

Crust:

1¾ cups	graham wafer crumbs	425 mL
½ cup	melted butter	125 mL
½ tsp.	cinnamon	2 mL
¼ cup	chopped nuts (optional)	50 mL

Filling:

2	eggs	2
8 oz.	pkg., cream cheese	250 g
½ cup	sugar	125 mL
1 tsp.	vanilla	5 mL
1½ cups	sour cream	375 mL

Topping:

2 cups	fresh OR frozen blueberries	500 mL
½ cup	sugar	125 mL
1 tbsp.	sugar	15 mL
4 tsp.	cornstarch	20 mL
	whipped cream (optional)	

Prepare crust by combining all ingredients. Press into the bottom of a 9" (2.5 L) springform pan. Prepare filling by blending all ingredients together until smooth. Pour over crust and bake at 350°F (180°C) for 50-60 minutes. Turn off heat and leave in oven until cool. Combine topping ingredients and cook until thickened. Cool and pour over cake. Cool in pan, in refrigerator, until topping is set. Remove sides of springform pan. Serve with whipped cream, if desired. **Serves:** 6-8.

Spicy Blueberry Puff

Fruit Base:

4 cups	blueberries	1 L
½ cup	water	125 mL
1 cup	sugar	250 mL

Dough:

1½ cups	flour	375 mL
2 tsp.	baking powder	10 mL
½ tsp.	salt	2 mL
½ cup	shortening	125 mL
¾ cup	milk	175 mL

Topping:

2 tbsp.	melted butter	25 mL
2 tbsp.	sugar	25 mL
½ tsp.	cinnamon	2 mL

Prepare the fruit base by placing the blueberries in the bottom of a deep baking dish. Pour the water over the berries and sprinkle on the sugar. Prepare the dough by combining the flour, baking powder and salt. Cut in the shortening. Add milk and stir with a fork to make a soft, sticky dough. Drop dough by spoonfuls on top of the fruit. Combine the topping ingredients. Make a hole in each lot of dough and pour topping mixture in each. Bake at 425°F (220°C) for 30-35 minutes. **Serves:** 6-8.

Cranberry Pork Chops

4-6	pork chops, 1" (2.5 cm) thick	4-6
	salt and pepper to taste (optional)	
2 cups	ground OR chopped cranberries	500 mL
¼-½ cup	honey	50-125 mL
¼ tsp.	ground cloves	1 mL
¼ tsp.	nutmeg	1 mL

Cranberry Pork Chops (Cont'd.)

Trim excess fat from chops. Dice the fat and melt 1 tbsp. (15 mL) of it over low heat in a frying pan. Brown chops in fat, seasoning with salt and pepper, if desired, then place in a shallow baking dish. Combine remaining ingredients, pour over chops and bake in a 300°F (150°C) oven for 1 hour. **Serving Suggestion:** Serve with Parslied Rice. **Serves:** 4-6. See photograph on front cover.

Cranberry Cheese Bread

1 cup	sugar	250 mL
1 cup	halved cranberries (or coarsely chopped)	250 mL
2 cups	flour	500 mL
1½ tsp.	baking powder	7 mL
½ tsp.	baking soda	2 mL
½ tsp.	salt	2 mL
1	orange, juice from, plus water to equal ¾ cup (175 mL)	1
2 tsp.	grated orange peel	10 mL
2 tbsp.	melted shortening	25 mL
1½ cups	shredded Cheddar cheese	375 mL
1	egg, beaten	1
½ cup	finely chopped walnuts	125 mL

Add ¼ cup (50 mL) of the sugar to the halved cranberries and let stand while preparing other ingredients. In a large bowl, combine flour, remaining sugar, baking powder, baking soda and salt. In a separate bowl, combine orange juice, peel, shortening, cheese and egg; mixing well. Pour orange mixture all at once into dry ingredients, mixing just until blended. Fold in cranberries and nuts and spread evenly in a 9 x 5'' (2 L) loaf pan. Bake at 350°F (180°C) for 1 hour. Remove from pan and cool. Best stored overnight before slicing. **Yield:** 1 loaf.

Orange Strudel Cranberry Coffee Cake

Batter:

½ cup	butter, softened	125 mL
1 cup	sugar	250 mL
2	eggs	2
1 tsp.	vanilla	5 mL
1 cup	sour cream	250 mL
1 tsp.	baking soda	5 mL
2 cups	flour	500 mL
½ tsp.	salt	2 mL
2 cups	coarsely chopped cranberries	500 mL
1	orange, grated rind of (optional)	1

Strudel:

¾ cup	brown sugar	175 mL
½ cup	flour	125 mL
1 tsp.	cinnamon	5 mL
¼ cup	butter	50 mL

Prepare batter by creaming the butter and sugar together. Add eggs and vanilla, beating well. In a separate bowl, combine the sour cream and baking soda. Add alternately to the batter with the flour and salt. Fold in the cranberries, and orange rind if desired. Blend all strudel ingredients together. Pour half the batter into a 9" (23 cm) springform pan or a 9 x 9" (2.5 L) baking dish. Sprinkle half the strudel on top. Cover with remaining batter and top with remaining strudel mixture. Bake at 350°F (180°C) for about 1 hour.
Serves: 6-8.

Cranberry Squares

Base:

½ cup	softened butter	125 mL
1 cup	flour	250 mL
2 tbsp.	icing sugar	25 mL

Filling:

2	eggs, beaten	2
1 cup	sugar	250 mL
½ cup	flour	125 mL
¼ tsp.	salt	1 mL
1 tsp.	baking powder	5 mL
1 tsp.	almond flavoring	5 mL
1 tsp.	vanilla extract	5 mL
½ cup	chopped dates OR raisins	125 mL
⅔ cup	cooked cranberries	150 mL
½ cup	shredded coconut	125 mL

Icing:

¼ cup	butter	50 mL
2 cups	icing sugar	500 mL
1	egg yolk	1
2 tsp.	milk	10 mL
1 tsp.	almond flavoring OR vanilla extract	5 mL

Combine all base ingredients and press into a 9 x 9" (2.5 L) baking dish. Prepare filling by combining the ingredients in order given. Spread over base and bake at 350°F (180°C) for 50 minutes. Prepare icing by beating butter until soft. Gradually add sugar, blending until creamy. Beat in egg yolk, milk and flavoring. Adjust sugar as necessary for good consistency. Spread icing over cooled square. **Yield:** 9 squares.

Spiced Currants

4 qts.	currants	4 L
2 cups	vinegar	500 mL
6 cups	sugar	1.5 L
1 tbsp.	ground cloves	15 mL
1 tbsp.	ground nutmeg	15 mL

Combine all ingredients in a large saucepan. Cook for 1 hour. Store in a tightly covered container in a cool place. **Yield:** 4 quarts (4 L).

Gooseberry Tarts

	baked tart shells	
2 cups	fresh gooseberries	500 mL
1 cup	boiling water	250 mL
⅔-1 cup	sugar OR to taste	150-250 mL
2 tbsp.	cornstarch	25 mL
1 tbsp.	butter	15 mL

Prepare tart shells. In a saucepan, cook berries with water until tender. Drain juice and return it to the saucepan. Add sugar and cornstarch, stirring well to combine. Add fruit and cook for 10 minutes. Stir in butter. Chill and pour into baked tart shells.

Huckleberry Jam

4 cups	huckleberries	1 L
3 cups	sugar	750 mL
2 tbsp.	lemon juice	25 mL
¼ tsp.	salt	1 ml

Wash and stem huckleberries, then place in a large saucepan. Add sugar, lemon juice and salt. Boil rapidly for 10 minutes or until thick. Skim, using a metal spoon. Pour into hot, sterilized jars and seal. **Yield:** Approximately 1 quart (1 L).

Pincherry Jelly

3 cups	prepared juice from 3 qts. (3L) fully-ripe pincherries	750 mL
6½ cups	sugar	1.625 L
1	bottle liquid fruit pectin	1
¼ tsp.	ground cloves (optional)	1 mL

Prepare the juice by adding 3 cups (750 mL) water to the pincherries. Bring to a boil and simmer, covered, for 15 minutes. Let drain in a jelly bag for several hours. Measure 3 cups (750 mL) juice into a large saucepan. Add exact amount of sugar, and cloves if desired. Bring to a boil. Stir in pectin and return to full rolling boil for 1 minute. Remove from heat, skim foam using a metal spoon and quickly fill sterilized jars. Seal. **Yield:** 5½ cups (1.375 L).

Raspberry Tarts

Pastry:

⅔ cup	butter	150 mL
½ cup	lightly packed brown sugar	125 mL
1	egg	1
1 tsp.	vanilla	5 mL
1½ cups	flour	375 mL

Filling:

⅓ cup	butter	75 mL
¼ cup	sugar	50 mL
1	egg	1
2 tsp.	lemon juice	10 mL
1½ tsp.	grated lemon rind	7 mL
½ cup	flour	125 mL
½ tsp.	baking powder	2 mL
4 tbsp.	raspberry jam	60 mL

Prepare pastry by creaming the butter and sugar together. Beat in egg and vanilla. Blend in the flour. Press into 12 ungreased, medium-sized muffin tins. Prepare filling by creaming together the butter and the sugar. Beat in the egg, lemon juice and grated rind. Blend the flour and baking powder together, then stir into the creamed mixture. Spoon 1 tsp. (5 mL) raspberry jam into each tart shell. Top with filling mixture, filling each tart about ⅔ full. Bake at 350°F (180°C) for 15-20 minutes or until golden. **Yield:** 12 tarts.

Raspberry Vinegar

6 cups	fresh OR frozen raspberries	1.5 L
3 cups	cider vinegar	750 mL
2 cups	sugar	500 mL

Place raspberries in a 2-quart (2 L) crock or jar (not plastic). Pour vinegar over berries and let stand overnight. Strain vinegar into a 1½-quart (1.5 L) saucepan, discarding the berries. Stir in the sugar. Bring to a boil and boil for 10 minutes. Pour hot vinegar into clean, sterilized bottles or jars and seal. Store several weeks in a cool place before using. **Serving Suggestion:** Add to a blend of oil and vinegar or to sour cream for a fruit salad dressing. **Yield:** Approximately 1 quart (1 L).

Irish Strawberry Pie

1	9" (23 cm) baked pastry shell	1
4 cups	frozen strawberries	1 L
1 cup	sugar	250 mL
¼ cup	water	50 mL
2½ tbsp.	cornstarch	35 mL
1 tbsp.	butter	15 mL
	whipped cream (optional)	

Prepare pastry. Combine berries and sugar. Let stand until berries thaw. Drain juice off and bring to a boil. Mix water, cornstarch and butter and add to juice. Cook for 2 minutes on low heat, covered. Cool slightly and then stir in strawberries. Pour into baked pastry shell. Chill. Serve topped with whipped cream, if desired. **Serves:** 6.

Strawberry Squares

Base:

1½ cups	graham wafer crumbs	375 mL
½ cup	melted butter	125 mL
2 tbsp.	sugar	25 mL

Filling and Topping:

2 cups	fresh OR frozen strawberries	500 mL
3 oz.	pkg., strawberry gelatin	85 g
½ cup	whipping cream	125 mL
½ cup	whipping cream	125 mL
2 tsp.	sugar	10 mL
½ tsp.	vanilla	2 mL
	graham wafer crumbs	

Prepare base by mixing all ingredients together. Press into an 8 x 8" (2 L) baking dish. Bake at 325°F (160°C) for 5 minutes. To prepare filling, bring berries to a boil in a saucepan. Add strawberry gelatin. Remove from heat and cool until partially set. Whip cream until stiff and fold into berry mixture. Spread over the base. Prepare the topping by whipping the second amount of cream. Add the sugar and vanilla. Spread over the filling. Sprinkle with wafer crumbs. Refrigerate for several hours before serving. **Serves:** 6-8.

Strawberry Bavarian Cream

10 oz.	pkg. frozen sliced strawberries, thawed	300 g
1 cup	boiling water	250 mL
3 oz.	pkg., strawberry gelatin	85 g
1 cup	whipping cream OR 1 pkg. dessert topping	250 mL

Drain strawberries, reserving juice. Dissolve gelatin in boiling water. Add cold water to reserved juice to equal 1 cup (250 mL) and stir it into the dissolved gelatin. Chill until almost set. In a bowl, beat cream until stiff. Beat gelatin until foamy. Fold berries and gelatin into the whipped cream. Pour into a 1-quart (1 L) mold or individual molds. Chill until firm. **Serves:** 6-8.

Strawberry Yum-Yums

1 cup	flour	250 mL
½ cup	butter	125 mL
¼ cup	packed brown sugar	50 mL
½ cup	chopped nuts	125 mL
2	egg whites	2
1 cup	sugar	250 mL
2 tsp.	lemon juice	10 mL
10 oz.	pkg. frozen strawberries, thawed	300 g
1 cup	whipping cream OR 1 pkg. dessert topping	250 mL

Combine flour, butter, brown sugar and nuts until crumbly. Press into an 8 x 8" (2 L) baking dish. Bake at 350°F (180°C) for 20-25 minutes. Cool; then break into crumbs and set aside. In a bowl, combine egg whites, sugar, lemon juice and strawberries. Beat at medium speed for 15-20 minutes. In a separate large bowl, whip the cream. Fold strawberry mixture into whipped cream. Put half the crumb mixture into the bottom of an 8 x 8" (2 L) greased baking dish. Spread strawberry mixture over crumbs. Top with remaining crumbs. Freeze. **Serves:** 8.

Prince Edward Island

Potato Perfect

Baked, mashed or French-fried — those are the ways most of us may think of using potatoes — but not the people of Prince Edward Island. The creative cooks of this province use the potato in everything from salads to main courses to desserts!

The distinctive red soil of Prince Edward Island has long been admired by tourists visiting the Island; but more than providing unique scenery, red soil also provides the rich mineral content that results in the unique taste that has made P.E.I. famous for its potatoes.

Somerset Maugham, the well-known author, attributed his longevity to eating potatoes twice daily. That particular claim might be difficult to prove but, in truth, the potato does provide excellent nutritional value, supplying vitamin C, vitamin B6 and iron, as well as many other minerals.

In spite of its great nutrition the potato has been much maligned over the years. This has been largely due to a lack of understanding. For example, many people assume the potato is a high-calorie, high-fat food. Not so! Potatoes are virtually fat-free and have no cholesterol. And there are only one hundred calories in one medium-size potato. It is the rich toppings that we often add to potatoes that add the calories.

As you read through the wonderful collection of potato recipes provided here, including the two traditional recipes, you'll be amazed at the versatility of this vegetable and at the imagination of Island cooks.

These recipes are all "potato perfect"!

Farmer's Breakfast, page 41

Potato Scones

1¼ cups	flour	300 mL
¼ cup	sugar	50 mL
3 tsp.	baking powder	15 mL
1 tsp.	salt	5 mL
⅓ cup	butter	75 mL
¼ cup	currants	50 mL
⅓ cup	milk	75 mL
1	egg, whole	1
1	egg, separated	1
¾ cup	mashed P.E.I. potatoes	175 mL
	sugar	

Combine the flour, sugar, baking powder and salt, mixing well. Cut in the butter until the mixture resembles coarse meal. Stir in the currants. Stir in the milk, the whole egg and 1 egg yolk. Add the potatoes. Stir with a fork until all the ingredients are well moistened. Turn dough onto a lightly floured board. Round up the dough and knead gently for about 20 strokes. Roll the dough, with a floured rolling pin, into a circle about ½" (1 cm) thick. Slightly beat the egg white, then brush it over the dough and sprinkle with sugar. Cut in 12 pie-shaped wedges and place on an ungreased baking sheet. Bake at 425°F (220°C) for 12-15 minutes. **Yield:** 12 scones.

Farmer's Breakfast

¼ lb.	bacon	125 g
1½ cups	hash brown potatoes	375 mL
1 cup	chopped onion	250 mL
2 tbsp.	chopped chives	25 mL
6	eggs, beaten	6
½ tsp.	salt	2 mL
¼ tsp.	pepper	1 mL
	grated cheese	

In a large cast-iron frying pan, fry the bacon. Add the potatoes, onion and chives. Cook for 5 minutes. Season beaten eggs with salt and pepper and stir into mixture in skillet. Sprinkle entire mixture with grated cheese. Cover and cook, over moderate heat, for 5 minutes. Loosen gently with spatula, cut into wedges and serve. **Serves:** 6 (generously). See photograph on page 40A.

Tangy Autumn Salad

Marinade:

¼ cup	vinegar	50 mL
½ cup	vegetable oil	125 mL
1	garlic clove, minced	1
1 tbsp.	sugar	15 mL
1 tsp.	salt	5 mL
¼ tsp.	pepper	1 mL
¼ tsp.	dry mustard	1 mL
¼ tsp.	dry tarragon	1 mL

Salad:

1 cup	thinly sliced carrots	250 mL
1	large P.E.I. potato, cubed	1
1 cup	turnip sticks	250 mL
1	small onion, sliced into rings	1
1 cup	broccoli florets	250 mL

Combine marinade ingredients in a small bowl and set aside. Cook the vegetables, except onion and broccoli, in boiling, salted water, until tender-crisp. Drain and cover immediately with very cold water. Drain again. Toss with onion rings and broccoli. Pour marinade over the vegetables. Cover and chill for several hours before serving. Serve on lettuce. **Serves:** 4-6.

Island Potato Soup

1	medium onion, finely chopped	1
3 tbsp.	butter	50 mL
2 tbsp.	chopped celery leaves	25 mL
3 cups	boiling water	750 mL
3	potatoes, peeled and cubed	3
dash	pepper	dash
1 tsp.	salt	5 mL
3 cups	scalded milk	750 mL

Island Potato Soup (Cont'd.)

Sauté onions in butter until lightly browned. Add celery leaves, boiling water, potatoes and seasonings. Cook until potatoes are tender, about 15 minutes. Add milk. Heat to boiling point, but do NOT let boil. **Serves:** 5.

Creamy Potato Soup

2 tbsp.	butter	25 mL
1	medium onion, finely chopped	1
3 cups	chicken stock	750 mL
3	medium potatoes, peeled and diced	3
2 cups	milk	500 mL
1 tbsp.	flour	15 mL
½ tsp.	salt	2 mL
	pepper to taste	
1½ cups	cooked, diced chicken	375 mL
1 tbsp.	finely chopped fresh parsley and chives	15 mL

Melt butter in a large saucepan. Add chopped onion and sauté gently for about 7 minutes or until transparent. Add chicken stock and potatoes. Cover and cook, over moderate heat, for about 20 minutes. Remove from heat. Mix a little of the milk with the flour to make a smooth paste and press out any lumps of flour. Combine the paste with the remaining milk, then add it to the mixture in the saucepan. Stir well and add the salt and pepper. Reheat soup to boiling, stirring continually as it thickens. When soup comes to a boil, add diced chicken and cook for an additional 5 minutes, over moderate heat, stirring occasionally. Stir in fresh chopped herbs just before serving. **Serves:** 4.

Crispy Potato Skins

6	medium potatoes	6
½ cup	melted butter	125 mL
1 tsp.	garlic salt	5 mL
¼ cup	grated Parmesan cheese	50 mL

Scrub potatoes and pat dry. Prick with a fork and bake at 400-450°F (200-230°C) for 40-60 minutes or until tender. Remove the potatoes and cut into quarters. Scoop out the pulp (save for hash browns or mash and use in baked products), leaving only a thin layer on each skin. Place skin-side down on a baking sheet and brush with the melted butter. Sprinkle with garlic salt. Bake at 350°F (180°C) for 20-25 minutes, until skins are brown and crisp. Add toppings, if desired. Sprinkle with cheese for the last 5 minutes of the cooking period. **Serves:** 6 as an appetizer.

Toppings:

3	bacon strips, cooked crisp and crumbled	3
¼ cup	grated Cheddar cheese	50 mL
¼ cup	chopped onion	50 mL
¼ cup	chopped green pepper, sautéed	50 mL
¼ cup	sliced fresh mushrooms, brushed with butter	50 mL

Top Crispy Potato Skins with any of the above.

Classy Baked Potatoes

potatoes, as many as
   required, scrubbed

Bases:

sour cream
cottage cheese and lemon
   juice, blended
mayonnaise
yogurt
cheese sauce, seasoned with
   paprika,
turmeric, rosemary, thyme
   and/OR dry mustard

Seasonings:

green onion, finely chopped
chives, finely chopped
parsley, finely chopped
celery, finely chopped
cucumber, finely chopped
radish, finely chopped
crisp bacon, crumbled
ham, finely chopped
chicken, finely chopped
cheese, grated
mushrooms, sliced and
   sautéed

Thoroughly scrub potatoes and pat dry. Prick with a fork, then bake at 400°F (200°C) for 1 hour. Cut 2 crossed gashes across each baked potato. Pinch potato to open cut and add any combination of the above bases and seasonings.

Golden Chicken Pie

2	9" (23 cm) single-crust Potato Pastry shells (see recipe, page 47)	2
3 lbs.	raw chicken, cut up	1.5 kg
1 tsp.	salt	5 mL
¼ tsp.	pepper	1 mL
3	carrots, sliced	3
4	celery stalks, chopped	4
1	large onion, chopped	1
3	P.E.I. potatoes, peeled and diced	3
½ cup	butter	125 mL
⅓ cup	flour	75 mL
½ cup	cream	125 mL
1 tsp.	salt	5 mL
¼ tsp.	pepper	1 mL
2 tbsp.	lemon juice	25 mL

Prepare pastry. Place chicken in a large saucepan. Cover with water and bring to a boil. Skim. Add first amount of salt and pepper. Lower heat and simmer for 30 minutes. Meanwhile, prepare vegetables and set aside. Strain chicken, reserving broth. Measure broth and add water to equal 3 cups (750 mL) of liquid. Place liquid in a saucepan, add vegetables and cook until tender, 10-12 minutes. Strain, again reserving stock. Bone and skin chicken and cut in bite-size pieces. Combine cooked vegetables and chicken and divide mixture between 2 deep, 9" (23 cm) pie plates. Melt butter in a saucepan, over medium heat. Gradually stir in flour, blending well. Cook for 1 minute, stirring constantly. Slowly add cream and cook until mixture is smooth and thick. Add second amount of salt and pepper, lemon juice and reserved stock; blend well. Pour half of the cream sauce over chicken-vegetable mixture in each pie plate and mix gently. Lay prepared potato pastry over the filling and press dough to sides of dish. Cut a slit in the center of pastry lid to allow steam to escape. Bake at 400°F (200°C) for about 30 minutes until the filling is bubbling and the crust is golden brown. **Yield:** 2 pies.

Potato Pastry

1½ cups	all-purpose flour	375 mL
½ tsp.	salt	2 mL
½ cup	lard	125 mL
¼ cup	mashed, P.E.I. potatoes	50 mL
1	egg yolk	1

Combine flour and salt and cut in lard, using 2 knives or a pastry cutter, until mixture is crumbly. Add mashed potatoes and egg yolk and toss with a fork (do not add water), until a ball is formed. Divide dough into 2 balls. Roll out pastry from center outward using light, even pressure, to form a circle 1" (2.5 cm) larger than the inverted pie plate, ⅛" (0.3 cm) thick. Place pastry in pie plate and trim. For a baked shell, prick dough all over with a fork and bake at 350°F (180°C) for 12-15 minutes. **Yield:** 2, 9" (23 cm) pie shells.

Cheesy Potato Casserole

7-8	medium potatoes, cooked and cubed OR 1 pkg. frozen hash browns	7-8
10 oz.	can, cream of mushroom soup	284 mL
1 cup	sour cream	250 mL
1 cup	grated Cheddar cheese	250 mL
⅓ cup	chopped onion	75 mL
⅓ cup	chopped green pepper	75 mL
	salt and pepper to taste	
	grated Parmesan cheese	
½ cup	crushed cornflakes	125 mL
¼ cup	melted butter	50 mL

Prepare potatoes. If using hash browns, thaw slightly for easier mixing. Combine the first 6 ingredients and season with salt and pepper. Spread potato mixture in a large, greased baking dish. Sprinkle with the Parmesan cheese. Top with the crushed cornflakes and drizzle with the melted butter. Bake at 350°F (180°C) for 45-60 minutes. **Serves:** 6-8.

P.E.I. Potato and Ham Casserole

2 cups	water	500 mL
1 tsp.	salt	5 mL
6 cups	raw potato slices, about 2½ lbs. (1 kg)	1.5 L
1 cup	sliced onion	250 mL
10 oz.	can, cream of mushroom soup	284 mL
1 cup	milk	250 mL
1 tbsp.	prepared mustard	15 mL
1 tbsp.	chopped parsley	15 mL
¼ tsp.	pepper	1 mL
2 cups	cubed, cooked ham	500 mL
	buttered bread crumbs	

Combine water and salt in a large saucepan, then bring to a boil. Add potatoes and onion. Cook 5 minutes. To make sauce, combine soup, milk, mustard, parsley and pepper. In a greased 8 x 12" (3 L) baking dish, layer ½ the potato-onion mixture with half of the ham. Cover with half of the sauce. Repeat layers. Top with buttered bread crumbs. Bake at 375°F (190°C) for 35-40 minutes, or until potatoes are fork-tender and sauce bubbles. **Serves:** 6-8.

Shepherd's Pie

1-1½ cups	ground beef	250-375 mL
2 tbsp.	flour	25 mL
1 cup	beef broth	250 mL
1 cup	cooked peas	250 mL
1 cup	cooked sliced carrots	250 mL
¾ cup	chopped onions	175 mL
	salt and pepper to taste	
1 cup	hot, mashed potatoes	250 mL
½ tsp.	salt	2 mL
1	egg	1
½ cup	milk	125 mL
1 tbsp.	butter	15 mL
½ tsp.	grated onion (optional)	2 mL

Shepherd's Pie (Cont'd.)

Prepare base by scramble-frying beef, until meat is no longer pink. Remove meat and set aside. Drain off all but 2 tbsp. (25 mL) of beef fat. Add flour to fat in frying pan and cook slightly. Gradually stir in beef broth. Cook until thickened to form gravy. Place meat, peas, carrots, onions, salt and pepper in layers in a large, buttered baking dish. Season with salt and pepper. Spread ¾ cup (175 mL) gravy over top. Combine mashed potatoes, salt, egg, milk, butter and grated onion and beat until fluffy. Spread over top of meat mixture and bake at 375°F (190°C) for 25 minutes, or until lightly browned.
Serves: 4.

Bran Muffins

½ cup	natural bran	125 mL
⅓ cup	sour milk	75 mL
½ cup	whole-wheat flour	125 mL
1 cup	all-purpose flour	250 mL
2 tsp.	baking powder	10 mL
1 tsp.	salt	5 mL
1 tsp.	baking soda	5 mL
½ cup	butter	125 mL
½ cup	brown sugar	125 mL
1	egg, beaten	1
½ cup	slightly warm, mashed P.E.I. potatoes	125 mL
½ cup	raisins	125 mL

Combine bran and sour milk and set aside for 10 minutes. In a separate bowl, combine the flours, baking powder, salt and baking soda. In a large bowl, cream butter and sugar together, then beat in egg and potatoes until smooth. Add the dry ingredients, the bran mixture and the raisins to the creamed mixture. Stir until well blended. Fill greased, or paper-lined, muffins tins ⅔ full and bake at 400°F (200°C) for 15-20 minutes or until muffins spring back when touched. **Yield:** 12 muffins.

Potato Bannock

2⅓ cups	flour	575 mL
1 tsp.	salt	5 mL
2 tbsp.	baking powder	25 mL
4 tbsp.	sugar	60 mL
2 tbsp.	shortening	25 mL
¾ cup	mashed P.E.I. potatoes	175 mL
1 cup	cold water	250 mL

Combine flour, salt, baking powder and sugar. Cut in shortening until the mixture resembles coarse meal. Stir in the potatoes. Stir in the cold water and mix, using a fork. Knead gently, 8-10 times, on a lightly floured board, working in any extra flour that may be required to overcome the stickiness of the dough. Place on an ungreased baking sheet and pat down to form an oval shape, about ¾-1'' (1.9-2.5 cm) in thickness. Bake at 450°F (230°C) for 17-20 minutes. Cut horizontally in slices. Serve hot or cold. **Serves:** 8-10.

Festival Cake

2 cups	sugar	500 mL
¾ cup	butter	175 mL
4	eggs, separated	4
2 cups	flour	500 mL
2 tsp.	baking powder	10 mL
1 tsp.	cinnamon	5 mL
1 tsp.	nutmeg	5 mL
¼ tsp.	salt	1 mL
1 cup	cocoa	250 mL
1 cup	raisins	250 mL
1 cup	mashed P.E.I potatoes	250 mL
1 tsp.	vanilla	5 mL
½ cup	milk	125 mL
1 cup	chopped walnuts	250 mL

Cream sugar and butter together well. Add egg yolks and beat. Combine dry ingredients. Flour raisins with ¼ cup (50 mL) of the dry ingredient mixture. Add potatoes to creamed mixture. Alternately add dry ingredients and milk, beginning and ending with flour. Add raisins, vanilla and nuts. Fold in stiffly beaten egg whites. Turn into a greased 10'' (3 L) tube pan and bake at 325°F (160°C) for about 1 hour. **Serves:** 8-10.

Potato Pound Cake

1 cup	butter, softened	250 mL
1 cup	sugar	250 mL
1 tsp.	grated lemon rind	5 mL
1 tbsp.	lemon juice	15 mL
4	eggs	4
³⁄₈ cup	finely mashed P.E.I. potatoes	75 mL
1⅝ cups	flour	400 mL
¼ tsp.	baking powder	1 mL
¼ tsp.	nutmeg (optional)	1 mL

Cream butter thoroughly, for 1 minute. Add sugar gradually, creaming well after each addition, beating for 10 minutes. Mix in the lemon rind and juice, beating for 30 seconds. Beat in the eggs, 1 at a time, beating 1½ minutes with each egg. Add the potatoes, mixing well. Combine the dry ingredients and stir into the potato mixture gradually. Mix just until smooth, about 1 minute. Pour into a greased and lightly floured 9 x 5 x 3" (2 L) loaf pan. Bake at 325°F (160°C) for about 60 minutes. Cool. Slice thinly and serve plain. **Note:** Beating for the specified amount of time is important for this cake's success. Pound cake is better if it is aged 1 or 2 days before serving. **Yield:** 1 loaf.

Grandma's Apple Cake

1¾ cups	flour	425 mL
½ tsp.	salt	2 mL
1 tbsp.	baking powder	15 mL
½ tsp.	cinnamon	2 mL
¾ cup	butter	175 mL
⅔ cup	sugar	150 mL
2	eggs, beaten	2
⅔ cup	hot, mashed P.E.I. potatoes	150 mL
2	cooking apples	2

Combine flour, salt, baking powder and cinnamon and set aside. Cream butter, sugar and eggs until light. Blend in potatoes. Fold flour mixture into creamed mixture, blending until mixed. Peel apples and slice thinly. (Do not do this beforehand, as apples will darken.) Fold apples into batter until blended. Turn batter into a greased and floured 8 x 8" (2 L) square baking pan. Bake at 350°F (180°C) for 45-50 minutes. **Serving Suggestion:** Serve with butter icing or whipped cream. **Yield:** 9 squares.

Potato Gingerbread

⅝ cup	shortening	175 mL
½ cup	sugar	125 mL
2	eggs	2
1 cup	molasses	250 mL
½ cup	finely mashed P.E.I. potatoes	125 mL
2⅛ cups	flour	525 mL
2 tsp.	baking powder	10 mL
1 tsp.	cinnamon	5 mL
1 tsp.	ginger	5 mL
½ tsp.	salt	2 mL
1 cup	hot water	250 mL

Cream shortening. Add sugar and cream together until well blended. Add eggs and molasses and beat thoroughly. Blend in potatoes. Combine flour, baking powder, cinnamon, ginger and salt. Add dry ingredients to the potato mixture and beat only until smooth. Add the hot water and mix until well blended. Turn batter into a lightly greased and floured 9 x 9'' (2.5 L) baking pan. Bake at 350°F (180°C) for about 40 minutes. **Serving Suggestion:** This gingerbread keeps well and may be served with whipped cream or foamy egg sauce. **Serves:** 8.

Rhubarb Potato Delight

Base:

3 cups	chopped fresh rhubarb, washed	750 mL
½ cup	sugar	125 mL
pinch	salt (optional)	pinch
	butter (optional)	

Topping:

1 cup	flour	250 mL
1½ tsp.	baking powder	7 mL
¼ tsp.	salt	1 mL
¼ cup	sugar	50 mL
⅜ cup	butter	75 mL
1 cup	riced P.E.I. potatoes (rice potatoes when hot)	250 mL

Rhubarb Potato Delight (Cont'd.)

Prepare base by placing rhubarb in a 9" (23 cm) pie plate. Add sugar, salt and dots of butter, if desired. Bake at 400°F (200°C) for 15 minutes. Prepare the topping by combining the flour, baking powder, salt and sugar. Cut in the butter. Stir in the potato. Knead to form a dough. Roll out to ½" (1 cm) thick on lightly floured board. Cut into rounds with a biscuit cutter. Remove fruit from oven. Drain off and reserve juice. Measure ¼ cup (50 mL) juice and pour back over the fruit. Cover rhubarb with rounds of biscuit topping. Bake at 400°F (200°C) for 15 minutes or until golden brown. Serve hot.
Serves: 6.

Fluffy Potato Doughnuts

3	eggs	3
1⅓ cups	sugar	325 mL
½ tsp.	vanilla	2 mL
1 cup	mashed OR riced P.E.I. potatoes	250 mL
2 tbsp.	melted shortening	25 mL
4 cups	flour	1 L
2 tbsp.	baking powder	25 mL
2 tsp.	nutmeg	10 mL
1 tsp.	salt	5 mL
½ cup	milk	125 mL
	sugar and cinnamon (optional)	

Beat eggs, sugar and vanilla until light in color. Blend in potatoes and shortening. Combine dry ingredients and add alternately with milk to the potato mixture. Mix well. Chill for 1 hour. On a lightly floured surface, roll dough to ½" (1 cm) thickness. Cut into doughnut shapes. Fry in hot fat, 375°F (190°C), for about 3 minutes, turning once. Drain. Dip in a mixture of sugar and cinnamon if desired. Serve warm. **Yield:** 2-2½ dozen doughnuts.

P.E.I. Drop Cookies

⅔ cup	butter	150 mL
1 cup	brown sugar	250 mL
1	egg, slightly beaten	1
2 tsp.	vanilla	10 mL
2 tsp.	grated orange rind	10 mL
1 cup	grated carrots	250 mL
½ cup	mashed P.E.I. potatoes	125 mL
1½ cups	flour	375 mL
1½ tsp.	baking powder	7 mL
¼ tsp.	salt	1 mL

Cream together the butter and brown sugar. Add the egg and vanilla and mix well. Beat in orange rind, carrot and mashed potatoes. Combine flour, baking powder and salt and add dry ingredients to the potato mixture. Drop by teaspoonfuls onto a greased baking sheet. Bake at 400°F (200°C) for 10-12 minutes. **Yield:** 40, 2" (5 cm) cookies.

Potato Fudge

1 cup	hot, mashed P.E.I. potatoes	250 mL
pinch	salt	pinch
2 tbsp.	butter	25 mL
4 cups	icing sugar	1 L
4 cups	unsweetened coconut	1 L
½ tsp.	vanilla	2 mL
½ cup	chopped cherries (optional)	125 mL
½ cup	chopped nuts (optional)	125 mL
½ cup	semisweet chocolate, melted	125 mL

Sprinkle the mashed potatoes with the salt and spread with the butter so that it melts. Add the icing sugar and stir until mixed. Add coconut, vanilla, and, optional ingredients if desired. Stir until well mixed, then pour mixture into a 9 x 13" (4 L) baking pan. Dribble melted chocolate over top. Allow to harden, then cut into squares to serve. **Yield:** 48, 1" (2.5 cm) squares.

New Brunswick

Out of the Shell

The province of New Brunswick makes a two-fold contribution to this cookbook as they present two of their local delicacies — shellfish and fiddleheads. The shores of this province have long been the landing site for a multitude of delicious shellfish — scallops, crabs, lobsters, oysters, clams and shrimp. And the W. I. cooks of New Brunswick have provided a collection of mouthwatering recipes to showcase these tempting foods. But, while New Brunswick is known for its shellfish, it is renowned for its unique edible fern — the fiddlehead. To quote Time Canada, "The fiddlehead is to New Brunswick what the maple leaf is to the rest of Canada, with one important difference. In addition to being a decorative symbol, the fiddlehead is a gastronomic delicacy."

Fiddleheads are the unfurled frond or leaf of the Ostrich Fern which commonly grows along many of New Brunswick's waterways. Picking fiddleheads has long been a spring tradition among New Brunswick families. As a rule, the ferns emerge within a week after flood waters have receded, between mid-May and mid-June.

So, for a real treat, come "out of your shell" today and try some taste-tempting recipes for shellfish and fiddleheads — yours from New Brunswick!

Seafood Casserole, page 67

New Brunswick Seafood Casserole

1½ cups	chicken broth OR 2 chicken bouillon cubes in 1½ cups (375 mL) water	375 mL
1 lb.	fresh OR frozen scallops	500 g
1 cup	fresh OR frozen oysters and juice	250 mL
	milk	
½ cup	butter	125 mL
¼ cup	chopped onion	50 mL
1½ cups	sliced fresh mushrooms	375 mL
½ cup	diced green pepper	125 mL
½ cup	flour	125 mL
1 cup	light cream	250 mL
½ tsp.	dry mustard	2 mL
1 tsp.	Worcestershire sauce	5 mL
1½ cups	fresh OR frozen cooked lobster	375 mL
½ lb.	fresh OR frozen shrimp, peeled, deveined and cooked	250 g
	salt and pepper to taste	
1-1½ cups	soft, buttered bread crumbs	250-375 mL

Bring chicken broth to a boil and add scallops. Cover and simmer for 5 minutes. Add oysters and juice. Cover and simmer until edges of oysters curl. Strain off liquid and measure. Add enough milk to make 2½ cups (625 mL) of liquid. Heat butter in a frying pan and add onion, mushrooms and green pepper. Sauté until onions are transparent. Remove from heat and stir in flour. Gradually add the liquid to the pan and stir to blend well. Return to the heat and cook until smooth and creamy, stirring almost continually. Add the cream, mustard and Worcestershire sauce. Reheat and add scallops, oysters, lobster and shrimp. Season with salt and pepper. Turn into a 2-quart (2 L) greased baking dish. Sprinkle with crumbs and bake at 375°F (190°C) until bubbly, about 35 minutes. **Serves:** 8-10.

Cream of Fiddlehead Soup

¾ cup	chopped green onion	175 mL
¼ cup	butter	50 mL
3 cups	chicken bouillon	750 mL
1½ cups	cubed potatoes	375 mL
1 lb.	fresh fiddleheads OR	500 g
	2 x 10 oz. (2 x 283 g) pkgs.	
	frozen fiddleheads	
½ tsp.	salt	2 mL
¼ tsp.	white pepper	1 mL
1⅔ cups	milk	400 mL
	chopped chives OR croutons	
	(optional)	

Sauté the onion in the butter for 5 minutes. Stir in the bouillon, potatoes, fiddleheads and seasonings. Cover and simmer until potatoes are tender, about 30 minutes. Purée in blender until smooth. Stir in milk. Serve hot or cold. Garnish with chopped chives or croutons, if desired. **Serves:** 8. See photograph on back cover.

Clam Appetizer Dip

1	garlic clove, halved	1
8 oz.	pkg. cream cheese	250 g
2 tbsp.	lemon juice	25 mL
1½ tbsp.	Worcestershire sauce	22 mL
½ tsp.	salt	2 mL
dash	pepper	dash
4 tbsp.	clam broth	60 mL
½ cup	minced, drained clams	125 mL

Rub a small bowl with the garlic halves, then discard the garlic. Place remaining ingredients in the bowl and blend well. Refrigerate for several hours before serving. **Serving Suggestion:** Serve with an assortment of crackers. **Yield:** Approximately 2 cups (500 mL) of dip.

Maritime Clam Chowder

10 oz.	can, clams and liquid	284 mL
¼ cup	finely diced salt pork	50 mL
¼ cup	chopped onion	50 mL
1 cup	diced raw potatoes	250 mL
2 cups	liquid (clam liquid plus water)	500 mL
2 cups	milk	500 mL
½ tsp.	salt	2 mL
dash	pepper	dash
1 tsp.	dried parsley	5 mL

Drain clams, reserving liquid. Rinse clams under cold running water and strain reserved liquid through cheesecloth to remove sand. Fry salt pork in a deep saucepan until crisp. Remove scraps from pan and save for use as garnish. Cook onion in fat until tender. Add potatoes and liquid. Cover and simmer for 10-15 minutes or until potatoes are tender. Add clams, milk, salt and pepper and simmer, but do NOT boil. When serving, add pork scraps and garnish with parsley. **Serves:** 6.

Crab Dip

1 cup	crab meat	250 mL
½ cup	mayonnaise	125 mL
¼ cup	vegetable oil	50 mL
1 tbsp.	sweet relish	15 mL
¼ tsp.	chopped parsley	1 mL
	salt and white pepper to taste	

Drain crab meat and remove any cartilage. Combine mayonnaise and vegetable oil. Add crab, relish and seasonings. Mix well and refrigerate. **Serving Suggestion:** Serve on a variety of crackers or bouches (tiny puff pastry patties). **Yield:** 1½ cups (375 mL) of dip.

Crab Casserole

10 oz.	can, cream of mushroom soup	284 mL
½ cup	milk	125 mL
8 oz.	pkg., processed cheese	250 g
½ cup	uncooked instant rice	125 mL
4.5 oz.	can, crab meat	120 g
	potato chips, crushed	

In a saucepan, combine soup and milk, then heat. Dice cheese, add to soup and stir until melted. Add the rice and crab, stirring well. Turn into a 2-quart (2 L) baking dish and sprinkle with crushed potato chips. Bake at 350°F (180°C) for 20-30 minutes or until bubbly. **Serves:** 6.

Crab and Shrimp Casserole

6.5 oz.	can, crab OR lobster, flaked	180 g
4.5 oz.	can, shrimp, cleaned and broken in pieces	120 g
1	medium green pepper, chopped	1
1	medium onion, chopped	1
1 cup	chopped celery	250 mL
½ tsp.	salt	2 mL
dash	pepper	dash
1 tsp.	Worcestershire sauce	5 mL
1 cup	mayonnaise	250 mL
1 cup	buttered bread crumbs	250 mL

Combine all ingredients, except bread crumbs, and mix well. Place in a greased 2-quart (2 L) baking dish. Sprinkle with crumbs. Bake at 350°F (180°C) for 30 minutes. **Serves:** 6.

Lobster Newburg

4 tbsp.	butter	60 mL
½ lb.	fresh mushrooms, sliced	250 g
3 tbsp.	flour	50 mL
½ tsp.	salt	2 mL
¼ tsp.	paprika	1 mL
¼ tsp.	dry mustard	1 mL
1½ cups	milk	375 mL
⅓ cup	shredded Cheddar cheese	75 mL
2	egg yolks, slightly beaten	2
2 x 6.5 oz.	cans, lobster meat, broken into bite-size pieces	2 x 180 g

Melt 2 tbsp. (25 mL) of the butter in a frying pan. Add the mushrooms and sauté until tender. In a saucepan, or double boiler, melt remaining butter. Blend in the flour, salt, paprika and mustard. Gradually add milk and stir constantly, cooking until smooth and thickened. Add cheese. Add a little sauce to slightly beaten egg yolks. Add egg mixture to the saucepan and cook for 2 minutes, stirring constantly. Add sautéed mushrooms and lobster meat. Heat thoroughly, stirring frequently. **Serving Suggestion:** Serve immediately over hot cooked rice or warm patty shells. Alternatively, Lobster Newburg may be placed in individual baking dishes and browned in a hot oven. **Serves:** 5-6.

Broiled Oysters

2 cups	fresh oysters, drained	500 mL
2 tbsp.	melted butter	25 mL
½ tsp.	salt	2 mL
1 tbsp.	lemon juice	15 mL
1 tbsp.	chopped parsley	15 mL
1	garlic clove, crushed	1
	lemon wedges	

Arrange oysters on a greased broiling pan. Combine butter, salt, lemon juice, parsley and garlic. Pour over oysters. Broil for 2-3 minutes or until edges begin to curl. Serve with lemon wedges. **Serves:** 4-6.

Oyster Dip

2 cups	shucked N.B. oysters	500 mL
4 oz.	pkg., cream cheese with onion	125 g
1 tbsp.	Worcestershire sauce	15 mL
¼ cup	whipping cream	50 mL
dash	dry mustard	dash
	salt to taste	
2 tbsp.	chopped parsley	25 mL

Simmer oysters in their liquid until edges curl. Drain and chop oysters coarsely. Blend all ingredients in a blender until smooth. Chill before serving. **Serving Suggestion:** Serve with a variety of fresh vegetables and crackers.
Yield: 3 cups (750 mL) of dip.

Oyster Stew

2 cups	fresh oysters	500 mL
6	bacon strips, diced	6
1 cup	chopped onion	250 mL
1 cup	diced celery	250 mL
2 cups	diced potatoes	500 mL
¾ cup	diced carrots	175 mL
1 cup	liquid (oyster liquid plus water)	250 mL
2 tsp.	salt	10 mL
½ tsp.	white pepper	2 mL
4 cups	milk	1 L
½ cup	dry white wine	125 mL
¼ cup	chopped parsley	50 mL

Simmer fresh oysters in their liquid for 3 minutes or until edges begin to curl. Drain oysters, reserving liquid. In a large saucepan, fry diced bacon until crisp. Remove bacon, reserving for garnish, and sauté onions in fat until golden brown. Add vegetables, liquid — add water to reserved oyster liquid to equal 1 cup (250 mL), salt and pepper. Cover and simmer for 15 minutes or until vegetables are tender. Stir in milk and just bring to a boil. Reduce heat. Add oysters and wine and heat through. Garnish with bacon bits and chopped parsley. **Serves:** 8, 1 cup (250 mL) each.

Coquilles Saint-Jacques

⅓ cup	finely chopped onion	75 mL
1 tbsp.	butter	15 mL
1½ tbsp.	finely chopped chives	22 mL
1	garlic clove, chopped	1
1½ lbs.	scallops, cut in ¼" (0.5 cm) slices)	750 g
	flour	
	salt and pepper to taste	
2 tbsp.	butter	25 mL
1 tbsp.	vegetable oil	15 mL
¾ cup	white wine	175 mL
½	bay leaf	½
dash	thyme	dash
	grated Swiss cheese	
	butter	

Sauté onions slowly in butter for 5 minutes or until transparent. Add chives and garlic and cook slowly for 1 minute. Coat the scallops in flour, salt and pepper, then quickly brown in a second pan with the butter and oil. Add onion mixture to the scallops. Add wine, bay leaf and thyme. Cover and simmer for 5 minutes. Remove bay leaf. Spoon scallops and sauce into buttered scallop shells. Sprinkle with grated cheese and dot with butter. Place under broiler for a few minutes, until golden brown. **Serves:** 4-6 as a main course, 8 as an appetizer.

Scallop Casserole

1 lb.	scallops	500 g
2	hard-cooked eggs, diced	2
1	small onion, chopped	1
10 oz.	can, cream of chicken OR cream of mushroom soup	284 mL
2 tbsp.	butter	25 mL
1½ tbsp.	flour	22 mL
1 cup	milk	250 mL
2 cups	bread crumbs, browned in butter	500 mL

Scallop Casserole (Cont'd.)

Add scallops to a saucepan containing cold water and bring to a near boil. Cook until tender, then drain. To the scallops, add eggs, onion and soup. Pour mixture into a buttered 2-quart (2 L) baking dish. Make a thin white sauce by melting the butter over medium heat. Stir in the flour until smooth. Gradually add the milk, stirring well to combine. Continue to cook over medium heat until the sauce is thickened, stirring constantly. Pour the sauce over the top of the scallop mixture in the casserole. Sprinkle generously with bread crumbs. Bake at 375°F (190°C) for 30-40 minutes. **Serves:** 4-6.

Curried Shrimp

¼ cup	melted butter	50 mL
¼ cup	flour	50 mL
½ tsp.	salt	2 mL
dash	paprika	dash
½-1 tsp.	curry powder	2-5 mL
1½ cups	milk	375 mL
3 tbsp.	ketchup	50 mL
¼ cup	cooking sherry	50 mL
2 lbs.	shrimp, shelled and cleaned	1 kg
2 cups	hot, cooked rice	500 mL
	chopped parsley	

In a saucepan, blend melted butter, flour and seasonings. Gradually stir in milk. Cook until thick and smooth, stirring constantly. Add ketchup, sherry and shrimp to the pan. Heat through. Serve over mounds of fluffy hot rice. Garnish with chopped parsley. **Serves:** 6.

Shrimp and Apple Salad

¾ lb.	cooked shrimp	375 g
2 cups	diced red apples, unpared	500 mL
1 tbsp.	lemon juice	15 mL
½ cup	chopped celery	125 mL
1 tsp.	salt	5 mL
½ cup	mayonnaise	125 mL
	lettuce cups	
	mayonnaise	
	pecan halves (optional)	

If shrimp are large, cut in half. Combine shrimp, apples, lemon juice, celery, salt and ½ cup (125 mL) mayonnaise and toss lightly to blend. Serve in lettuce cups. Garnish with mayonnaise and pecan halves, if desired. **Serves:** 4.

Seafood Muffins

1 cup	small shrimp, drained and coarsely chopped	250 mL
¼ cup	shredded old Cheddar cheese	50 mL
⅓ cup	sour cream	75 mL
¼ cup	finely chopped celery	50 mL
1½ cups	flour	375 mL
2 tbsp.	sugar	25 mL
2 tsp.	baking powder	10 mL
½ tsp.	salt	2 mL
¼ tsp.	thyme	1 mL
1	egg	1
¾ cup	milk	175 mL
⅓ cup	vegetable oil	75 mL
	fresh parsley, snipped	

Combine shrimp, cheese, sour cream and celery. Set aside. In a bowl, combine flour, sugar, baking powder, salt and thyme. Make a well in center of dry ingredients. In a second bowl, slightly beat the egg with a fork. Beat in milk and oil. Add egg mixture to well in dry ingredients and stir just until moist. Spoon into well-greased muffin tins and top with shrimp mixture, about 1 tbsp. (15 mL) per muffin. Bake at 375°F (190°C) for 20 minutes. Garnish with snipped parsley and serve warm. **Yield:** 12 muffins.

Seafood Casserole

2 lbs.	cooked seafood (any combination of lobster, crab, shrimp, cod, haddock)	1 kg
	boiling water	
2 cups	fish OR chicken bouillon	500 mL
6 tbsp.	butter	90 mL
6 tbsp.	flour	90 mL
1 cup	light cream	250 mL
2	egg yolks	2
1 cup	sliced mushrooms	250 mL
1 tbsp.	butter	15 mL
½ cup	grated Cheddar cheese	125 mL
2 tbsp.	chopped pimiento	25 mL
1 tbsp.	lemon juice	15 mL
pinch	cayenne pepper	pinch
	salt and pepper to taste	
1 cup	bread cubes	250 mL
2 tbsp.	melted butter	25 mL

Thaw any frozen fish, then drain well. Remove any cartilage and break fish into chunks. Poach fish fillets in boiling water for 8-10 minutes or until fish flakes easily. Drain and reserve liquid. Add enough bouillon to the cooking liquid to make 2 cups (500 mL). In a large saucepan, melt 6 tbsp. (90 mL) butter and blend in flour. Gradually add liquid and heat, stirring until thickened. Combine egg yolks and cream and add slowly to sauce, stirring constantly until thickened and smooth. Sauté mushrooms in 1 tbsp. (15 mL) butter. Add mushrooms, cheese, pimiento, lemon juice, cayenne and all seafood to sauce. Season with salt and pepper. Pour mixture into a lightly greased 2-quart (2 L) baking dish. Toss bread crumbs in the 2 tbsp. (25 mL) melted butter and sauté until bread cubes are golden brown. Sprinkle bread cubes on casserole. Bake in a 375°F (190°C) oven for 30-40 minutes, until bubbly. **Serving Suggestion:** This casserole can be frozen for later use. This sauce does not separate. **Serves:** 8. See photograph page 56A.

Seafood Scallop

4 tbsp.	melted butter	60 mL
4 tbsp.	flour	60 mL
½ tbsp.	dry mustard	7 mL
	salt and pepper to taste	
1 cup	milk	250 mL
½ cup	mayonnaise OR salad dressing	125 mL
dash	Tabasco sauce	dash
1 lb.	scallops	500 g
1 lb.	lobster OR shrimp	500 g
10 oz.	can, mushroom soup	284 mL
	cornflake crumbs	
	butter	

In a saucepan, melt the 4 tbsp. (60 mL) butter. Blend in the flour, mustard, salt and pepper. Add milk gradually and cook over medium heat, stirring constantly until smooth and thick. In a buttered 2-quart (2 L) baking dish, combine the mayonnaise, Tabasco sauce, scallops, lobster and soup. Add the white sauce and stir to combine. Cover with cornflake crumbs and dot with butter. Bake at 400°F (200°C) for 45 minutes. **Serves:** 8.

Shellfish Chowder

	butter	
¼ lb.	bacon, diced	100 g
1	onion, diced	1
4 cups	diced potatoes	1 L
	water	
4 cups	milk	1 L
½ lb.	fish fillets	250 g
½ lb.	scallops	250 g
4.5 oz.	can, lobster and juice	120 g
4 oz.	can, shrimp and juice	113 g
10 oz.	can, cream of mushroom soup	284 mL
	salt and pepper to taste	

Shellfish Chowder (Cont'd.)

Melt the butter in a large saucepan. Fry bacon in the butter until crisp. Add onion, potatoes and enough water to barely cover them. Boil for 10 minutes. Add milk and bring to a simmer. Add fillets, scallops, lobster and shrimp. Cook for an additional 10 minutes. Add soup, salt and pepper. Heat through, then serve. **Serves:** 8-10.

Fiddlehead Quiche

1	**9" (23 cm) unbaked pastry shell**	1
	flour	
3	**eggs**	3
1 cup	**cooked fiddleheads**	250 mL
1 cup	**chopped fresh mushrooms**	250 mL
1 cup	**grated Cheddar cheese**	250 mL
2 tbsp.	**chopped green onion**	25 mL
⅔ cup	**milk**	150 mL
	salt and pepper to taste	
	paprika to taste	
3	**bacon slices, cooked crisp and crumbled**	3

Sprinkle pastry shell with flour. Beat eggs. Add fiddleheads, mushrooms, cheese, onion, milk and seasonings. Pour into pastry shell. Top with crumbled bacon. Bake at 375°F (190°C) for 35-40 minutes, or until top is golden brown. **Serves:** 6.

Gourmet-Style Marinade for Fiddleheads

2 tbsp.	olive oil	25 mL
¼ cup	wine vinegar	50 mL
½ cup	water	125 mL
1 tsp.	lemon juice	5 mL
¼ tsp.	salt	1 mL
	fresh parsley	
	thyme	
5	peppercorns	5
1	rosemary sprig, tied in a bag	1
1	garlic clove, crushed	1
2	green onions, chopped	2
1 cup	fresh fiddleheads	250 mL

Bring first 9 ingredients to an aromatic boil, then reduce heat and simmer for 5 minutes. Increase heat again and add garlic, green onions and fiddleheads. Boil for 1 minute, then remove from heat and allow to cool completely, about 1-2 hours. Remove bag of rosemary. Store in a covered glass bowl in the refrigerator for up to 2 weeks. **Yield:** 2 cups (500 mL).

Marinade For Fiddleheads

½ cup	vegetable oil	125 mL
½ cup	vinegar	125 mL
1	onion, chopped	1
1	garlic clove, chopped	1
	parsley and dill to taste	
	fresh fiddleheads	
1 cup	water	250 mL

Combine all ingredients, except fiddleheads and water. Wash fiddleheads under running water until all brown scaly coverings have been removed. Place in a small saucepan with water, cover and simmer until just tender, about 10 minutes. Pour marinade over cooked, drained fiddleheads. Chill until ready to serve.

Quebec

Ways With Vegetables

FOR HOME AND COUNTRY

"Eat all your vegetables and you'll get a treat." Who amongst us hasn't heard or said that at some time? Well, the W.I. cooks of Quebec have solved the problem — they have made the vegetables, themselves, the treat! With the innovative recipes in this section, you will have no trouble getting people to eat their veggies, that's for sure!

Vegetables are among the most nutritious of foods. As a group, they are the greatest source of vitamins in our diets. They also have the added bonus of being low in calories. There are dozens of different varieties to choose from and there are many different ways to prepare them, as you will soon see.

One uniquely Canadian dish is vegetables glazed with maple syrup. The sweet maple flavor perfectly accents the simplicity of most vegetables. Quebec cooks are most familiar with the versatility of maple products. Maple syrup, the natural sweetener, is produced by the sugar maple tree which is found only in North America. Canada claims 70% of the world's maple production. Of this, Quebec is by far the largest producer.

Early settlers to Quebec learned from the Native people to extract the sap from the maple tree and to boil it down to syrup and sugar. For centuries, the melting snow and flowing sap have signalled a mouth-watering sign of spring and the return of that unique maple flavor. Years ago, children and adults alike looked forward to spending at least one afternoon in the sugar camp when the local sugarmaker "sugared off". Though the technology of sugar making has advanced considerably, many people retain this tradition. It is incredible to note that it takes thirty to forty gallons of sap to make just one gallon of that precious maple syrup.

For your enjoyment, two traditional Quebec maple recipes have been included here. Of course, you may want to experiment with maple syrup and the vegetables of your province. Then, move on to an array of vegetable recipes. You are sure to agree that our Quebec cooks have a "way with vegetables".

Quebec Baked Beans, page 73
Corn Fritters, page 77

Quebec Baked Beans

4 cups	beans	1 L
1 tsp.	baking soda	5 mL
½ cup	salt pork	125 mL
½ cup	molasses	125 mL
1 cup	maple syrup OR brown sugar	250 mL
1 tsp.	mustard	5 mL
2	medium onions, finely chopped	2
	salt and pepper to taste	
1 cup	chili sauce	250 mL

Soak beans in cold water overnight. In the morning, cover with fresh water and rinse. Repeat several times. Place beans in a large saucepan, add baking soda to fresh water and pour over beans. Boil until soft enough to break. Rinse again several times. Put beans in a bean pot, or casserole dish, layering alternately with pork. Combine remaining ingredients, except chili sauce, and add enough water so mixture covers the beans. Bake, covered, at 250°F (120°C) for 6-7 hours. Add chili sauce during last hour of baking. **Serves:** 8-10. See photograph on page 72A.

Quebec French Toast

5	eggs	5
¼ cup	milk	50 mL
4 tbsp.	maple syrup	60 mL
¼ tsp.	cinnamon	1 mL
¼ tsp.	freshly ground nutmeg	1 mL
dash	salt	dash
dash	pepper	dash
10 tbsp.	butter	150 mL
10	bread slices	10

Beat eggs for 3 minutes in a large bowl. Add milk, maple syrup and spices. Beat again until blended. Melt 1 tbsp. (15 mL) of the butter in a frying pan. Dip 1 slice of bread in the egg mixture. Fry bread on both sides until golden brown. Repeat with remaining bread slices using 1 tbsp. (15 mL) butter for each slice. **Serving Suggestion:** Serve hot with maple syrup. **Serves:** 4-5.

Asparagus Au Gratin

½ lb.	fresh asparagus	250 g
½ tsp.	salt	2 mL
1 cup	water	250 mL
2 tbsp.	butter	25 mL
2 tbsp.	flour	25 mL
	salt and pepper to taste	
1 cup	milk	250 mL
2	hard-cooked eggs, sliced	2
1 cup	grated Cheddar cheese	250 mL
¼ cup	bread crumbs	50 mL

Cut asparagus in 1'' (2.5 cm) pieces and cook in salted water for about 10 minutes. Drain well. Melt butter and blend in flour, salt and pepper. Add milk slowly and cook until thick and smooth, stirring constantly. Arrange asparagus, eggs, cheese and sauce in layers in a baking dish. Sprinkle crumbs over top. Bake at 350°F (180°C) for 30 minutes. **Serves:** 4.

Chinese Asparagus

2 tbsp.	butter	25 mL
1 lb.	fresh asparagus, chopped	500 g
½ cup	sliced green onion	125 mL
½ cup	quartered mushrooms	125 mL
2	chicken bouillon cubes dissolved in 1 cup (250 mL) hot water	2
1 tbsp.	brown sugar	15 mL
1 tbsp.	soy sauce	15 mL
¼ cup	cold water	50 mL
2 tbsp.	cornstarch	25 mL

Heat the butter in a wok or frying pan. Add vegetables and stir-fry until tender-crisp. To make the sauce, dissolve the bouillon cubes in the hot water in a saucepan. Add brown sugar and soy sauce. Combine cold water and cornstarch and stir until smooth, then add to bouillon mixture. Bring to a boil and boil for 3 minutes, stirring as it thickens. Add sauce to stir-fried vegetables and serve at once. **Serves:** 6. See photograph front cover.

Bean Salad

Salad:

10 oz.	can, green beans	284 mL
10 oz.	can, yellow beans	284 mL
10 oz.	can, lima beans	284 mL
10 oz.	can, kidney beans	284 mL
1	cucumber, chopped	1
2	medium onions, sliced	2

Dressing:

½ cup	vegetable oil	125 mL
½ cup	vinegar	125 mL
½ cup	sugar	125 mL
1 tsp.	salt	5 mL
½ tsp.	dry mustard	2 mL
	salt and pepper to taste	
1	garlic clove, minced	1

Drain canned beans. Combine beans, cucumber and onions in a large bowl. Combine all dressing ingredients and pour over salad. Let stand, refrigerated, 24 hours before serving. **Serves:** 8-10.

Glazed Broccoli Stems

7	broccoli stems, peeled and sliced	7
10 oz.	can, chicken broth	284 mL
1 tbsp.	fresh lemon juice	15 mL
2 tbsp.	unsalted butter	25 mL
1 tbsp.	chopped parsley	15 mL
	pepper to taste	

In a saucepan, combine broccoli and broth. Bring to a boil and simmer, covered, for 10-12 minutes. Transfer broccoli, using a slotted spoon, to a bowl. To liquid left in the pan, add the lemon juice and boil until liquid is reduced to ¼ cup (50 mL). Stir in butter, parsley and pepper. Add broccoli and stir to coat. **Serves:** 4.

Baked Broccoli

	boiling, salted water	
2 cups	chopped fresh broccoli OR cauliflower	500 mL
½ cup	chopped onion	125 mL
½ cup	chopped green pepper	125 mL
1 cup	shredded Cheddar cheese	250 mL
1½ cups	milk	375 mL
¾ cup	biscuit mix	175 mL
3	eggs	3
1 tsp.	salt	5 mL
¼ tsp.	pepper	1 mL

Heat 1'' (2.5 cm) salted water, ½ tsp. (2 mL) salt to 1 cup (250 mL) water, to boiling. Add broccoli, cover and return to a boil, cooking until almost tender, about 5 minutes. Drain thoroughly. Combine broccoli, onion, green pepper and cheese in a pie plate. Beat remaining ingredients until smooth; 15 seconds in blender on HIGH or 1 minute with hand mixer. Pour over broccoli mixture. Bake at 400°F (200°C) for 35-40 minutes. Remove when knife inserted in the center comes out clean. Let stand for 5 minutes before serving. **Serves:** 6.

Maple-Glazed Carrots

1 lb.	carrots, cut into 2'' (5 cm) pieces	500 g
2 tbsp.	butter	25 mL
2 tbsp.	packed brown sugar	25 mL
2 tbsp.	maple syrup	25 mL
¼ tsp.	ground ginger	1 mL
¼ tsp.	salt	1 mL
dash	white pepper	dash

Cook carrots in water until tender-crisp. In a small saucepan, combine the butter, sugar, maple syrup, ginger, salt and pepper. Cook; bring to a boil, stirring often. Pour over cooked carrots, tossing to coat. **Serves:** 4-6.

Marinated Carrots

2 lbs.	carrots, thinly sliced, cooked until tender-crisp	1 kg
1	onion, thinly sliced	1
1	green pepper, thinly sliced	1
10 oz.	can tomato soup	284 mL
½ cup	vegetable oil	125 mL
1 cup	sugar	250 mL
¼ cup	vinegar	50 mL
1 tsp.	salt	5 mL
½ tsp.	celery seed	2 mL

Combine carrots, onion and green pepper, set aside. Combine all marinade ingredients and bring to a boil in a saucepan. Pour over vegetables and refrigerate for at least 24 hours before serving. **Serves:** 8-10.

Corn Fritters

1½ cups	flour	375 mL
2 tsp.	baking powder	10 mL
⅓ cup	butter	75 mL
1	egg, slightly beaten	1
1 cup	milk OR juice from canned corn	250 mL
1 cup	fresh OR canned kernel corn	250 mL
½ tsp.	salt	5 mL
	pepper to taste	
	vegetable oil	

Combine flour and baking powder. Cut in butter. Add egg and milk or juice all at once to flour mixture. Combine corn, salt and pepper and add to batter, mixing well. Heat vegetable oil to 375°F (190°C). Drop batter by spoonfuls into hot fat and fry until golden. Drain on paper towels before serving. **Serving Suggestion:** These may be served with honey and chicken or with gravy and roast beef or pork. **Serves:** 4. See photograph on page 72A.

Parsnip Pie

Filling:

1	9" (23 cm) baked pastry shell	1
4	parsnips, sliced	4
1 cup	milk	250 mL
¼ cup	liquid honey	50 mL
2	eggs, slightly beaten	2
½ tsp.	grated orange rind	2 mL
½ tsp.	cinnamon	2 mL
pinch	allspice	pinch

Topping:

2 tbsp.	liquid honey	25 mL
1 cup	whipping cream, whipped	250 mL
	cinnamon	

Prepare pastry shell and and set aside to cool. Cook parsnips until tender, about 10 minutes. Drain and purée. Measure 2½ cups (625 mL) purée and add milk, honey, eggs, rind and spices, mixing well. Pour into cooled pastry shell. Bake at 375°F (190°C) for about 50 minutes until filling is set. Remove pie from oven and spread the 2 tbsp. (25 mL) of honey on top. Garnish with whipped cream and sprinkle with cinnamon. **Serves:** 6.

Cheesy Chive Potatoes

3	medium potatoes, peeled and boiled	3
½ cup	cottage cheese	125 mL
1 tbsp.	chopped chives	15 mL
¼ tsp.	salt	1 mL
pinch	freshly ground pepper	pinch

Potatoes should be warm. If using refrigerated potatoes, place in a steamer over boiling water for about 10 minutes. In warm, ovenproof bowl, roughly mash potatoes. Stir in cottage cheese, chives, salt and pepper. Serve immediately or keep warm in 200°F (100°C) oven until serving time. **Serves:** 4.

Scalloped Potatoes

10 oz.	can cream of celery soup	284 mL
½ cup	milk	125 mL
dash	Worcestershire sauce	dash
	salt and pepper to taste	
4 cups	peeled and thinly sliced potatoes	1 L
½ cup	sliced onions	125 mL
1 cup	shredded cheese	250 mL
1 tbsp.	butter	15 mL

Combine soup, milk, Worcestershire sauce, salt and pepper to make a sauce. In a large, buttered baking dish, layer potatoes, onion and cheese. Pour sauce over top. Dot with butter. Bake, covered, at 375°F (190°C) for 1 hour. Remove cover and bake for an additional 15 minutes. **Serves:** 6.

Rice and Tomato Casserole

½ cup	uncooked instant rice	125 mL
1 tsp.	salt	5 mL
3 tbsp.	flour	50 mL
¼ tsp.	pepper	1 mL
1 tsp.	chili powder	5 mL
2 tbsp.	butter	25 mL
1 lb.	ground beef	500 g
2 tbsp.	chopped onion	25 mL
28 oz.	can, tomatoes, including liquid	796 mL
12 oz.	can, kernel corn, including liquid	341 mL

Grease a baking dish. Put rice in bottom of dish. Combine salt, flour, pepper and chili powder. Sprinkle ⅓ of salt mixture over rice. Dot with butter. Mix beef and onion and spread over rice. Repeat ⅓ salt mixture. Add tomatoes and last ⅓ of salt mixture. Dot with butter. Put corn on top. Grease cover well. Bake, covered, at 350°F (180°C) for 45-50 minutes. **Serves:** 4-6.

Tomato-Cheese Bake

4	large tomatoes, sliced	4
	salt and pepper to taste	
½ cup	mayonnaise	125 mL
6	green onions, chopped	6
1 cup	grated Cheddar cheese	250 mL
1 cup	grated mozzarella cheese	250 mL

In a baking dish, arrange sliced tomatoes. Sprinkle with salt and pepper. Spread mayonnaise over tomatoes and top with chopped onions. Cover with the grated cheeses. Bake at 350°F (180°C) for 25 minutes. **Serves:** 6.

Turnip Soufflé Casserole

2 tbsp.	butter	25 mL
2-3 tbsp.	flour	25-50 mL
1 cup	milk	250 mL
1 cup	cooked, mashed turnip	250 mL
2-3 tbsp.	chopped onion	25-50 mL
2 tsp.	lemon juice	10 mL
¼ tsp.	salt	1 mL
	pepper to taste	
dash	Worcestershire sauce	dash
3	egg yolks, beaten	3
3	egg whites, stiffly beaten	3

Make a heavy white sauce by melting the butter over medium heat. Stir in the flour and when bubbly, slowly incorporate the milk. Cook, stirring constantly, until the mixture boils and is thickened. Combine the mashed turnips with the white sauce. Let cool, then mix in onion, lemon juice, salt, pepper and Worcestershire sauce. Add the beaten egg yolks and fold in the stiffly beaten egg whites. Turn into a greased soufflé or baking dish and place in a pan of hot water. Bake at 325°F (160°C) for about 1 hour. **Serves:** 6.

Scalloped Turnip with Apple

4 cups	sliced, cooked turnips	1 L
2 cups	peeled, sliced, uncooked apples	500 mL
¼ cup	brown sugar	50 mL
1 tsp.	salt	5 mL
¼ cup	butter	50 mL
½ cup	buttered bread crumbs	125 mL

Place 2 cups (500 mL) turnip in a greased baking dish. Cover with 1 cup (250 mL) apple slices. Sprinkle half the sugar and salt over apples in dish. Dot with half the butter. Repeat these layers. Bake, covered, at 350°F (180°C) until apples are tender, about 20-30 minutes. Uncover, sprinkle with bread crumbs and bake about 10 minutes or until lightly browned. **Serving Suggestion:** Good with poultry or pork. **Serves:** 6.

Easy Zucchini Casserole

zucchini, sliced
tomatoes, sliced
onions, sliced
salt and pepper to taste
additional seasonings as
    desired (e.g. basil,
    oregano, dillweed, etc.)
cheese slices
leftover cooked meat
    (optional)

All quantities may be varied depending on availability and on number of servings required. Layer slices of zucchini, tomatoes and onions, seasoning each layer as desired. Add cheese slices over each layer, finishing with a layer of cheese. Meat may be added if desired. Bake at 375°F (190°C) for 35-40 minutes.

Down-East Veggie Chowder

3 tbsp.	butter	50 mL
½ cup	chopped onion	125 mL
1 cup	chopped carrots	250 mL
1½ cups	chopped potatoes	375 mL
1 tsp.	salt	5 mL
¼ tsp.	nutmeg	1 mL
¼ tsp.	pepper	1 mL
2 tsp.	instant chicken bouillon mix	10 mL
¼ tsp.	garlic powder	1 mL
1 cup	water	250 mL
½ cup	chopped broccoli OR other green vegetable	125 mL
1 tbsp.	cornstarch	15 mL
2 cups	milk	500 mL
2 tbsp.	sour cream OR plain yogurt snipped parsley, chopped chives OR croutons	25 mL

Melt butter in a large, heavy saucepan. Add onion, carrot, potatoes and seasonings. Add water. Cover pan and simmer gently for 10 minutes. Add broccoli and simmer 5 minutes longer. Transfer broccoli to a blender, add cooking water and blend to desired consistency. Return to saucepan. Mix cornstarch and milk, add to vegetable mixture in pan and heat slowly for 2 minutes or until thickened. Add sour cream or yogurt. Serve, garnished with parsley, chives or croutons. Serve hot or cold. **Serves:** 6, 1 cup (250 mL) each.

Italian Medley
(microwave recipe)

2 cups	thinly sliced zucchini	500 mL
1	small onion, thinly sliced in rings	1
2 tbsp.	water	25 mL
1	tomato, cut in wedges	1
1 tbsp.	butter	15 mL
½ tsp.	dried parsley flakes	2 mL
½ tsp.	lemon juice	2 mL
¼ tsp.	salt*	1 mL
¼ tsp.	dried crushed basil	1 mL

In a pie plate or small baking dish, combine zucchini, onion and water. Cover and microwave on HIGH (full power) for 2-3 minutes. Add tomato wedges. Cover and microwave on HIGH for 1-2 minutes. Drain. Gently stir in butter, parsley, lemon juice, salt and basil. ***Note:** Don't add salt to food during microwave cooking time, as it toughens food. Microwaved foods also require less salt as foods retain more of their natural flavors. **Serves:** 4.

Chicken and Vegetable Casserole

2 cups	cooked, diced chicken	500 mL
3	hard-cooked eggs, sliced	3
2 tbsp.	chopped celery	25 mL
1 tbsp.	finely chopped onion	15 mL
10 oz.	can, sliced mushrooms, drained	284 mL
10 oz.	can, peas, drained	284 mL
10 oz.	can, cream of chicken soup	284 mL
½ cup	mayonnaise	125 mL
	chow mein noodles	

In a greased baking dish, combine chicken, eggs, celery, onion, mushrooms, peas, chicken soup and mayonnaise. Mix well. Sprinkle noodles over the top and bake at 350°F (180°C) for 30 minutes. **Serves:** 6.

Hearty Stew

2 tbsp.	butter	25 mL
2 lbs.	beef, cubed	1 kg
8 cups	water	2 L
1	garlic clove, minced	1
1	leek, diced	1
2	celery stalks, diced	2
6	large carrots, diced	6
4	large potatoes, peeled and cubed	4
2 tsp.	salt	10 mL
¼ tsp.	freshly ground pepper	1 mL
1 cup	pearl barley	250 mL

In a large soup pot, heat butter. Add beef and cook, stirring, until beef is lightly browned all over. Add water and simmer. Add garlic, leek, celery, carrots and potatoes. Season with salt and pepper. Simmer for 30 minutes. Stir in barley and continue to simmer until barley is tender and stew thickens, about 1 hour. **Serves:** 8.

Celebrity Recipes

Hon. John Wise
Minister, Agriculture Canada

Canadian Swiss Potato Soup

2 tbsp.	butter	25 mL
¼ cup	chopped onion	50 mL
2 cups	diced raw potatoes	500 mL
1 cup	boiling water	250 mL
1 tsp.	salt	5 mL
dash	marjoram	dash
3	chicken bouillon cubes	3
3 cups	milk	750 mL
2 tbsp.	flour	25 mL
1 tbsp.	chopped parsley	15 mL
1 cup	shredded Canadian-made Swiss cheese	250 mL

In a large saucepan, melt butter and sauté onion until tender. Add potatoes, water, salt, marjoram and bouillon cubes. Cover and simmer for 10 minutes, or until potatoes are tender. Combine milk and flour. Stir into potato mixture. Cook over medium heat, stirring constantly, until thickened and boiling. Stir in parsley. Top each serving with cheese. **Serves:** 4.

Hon. Brian Peckford
Premier of Newfoundland

Broiled Fresh Codfish

3 tbsp.	margarine	50 mL
3 lbs.	fresh codfish	1.5 kg
	salt and pepper to taste	
1	large onion, sliced	1
4	bacon strips	4
1	lemon, cut in wedges	1

Place ½ the margarine in a shallow baking dish. Add fresh codfish in a single layer and season with salt and pepper. Spread onion slices over fish, then top with remaining margarine and bacon strips. Bake at 375°F (190°C) for 15 minutes. Serve with lemon wedges. **Serves:** 6.

Hon. Roger Bacon
Nova Scotia Minister of Agriculture

Blueberry Crumble

Fruit Base:

1 tsp.	lemon juice	5 mL
4 cups	fresh OR dry pack	1 L
	blueberries, rinsed, drained	
½ cup	sugar	125 mL
2 tbsp.	flour	25 mL

Topping:

1¼ cups	quick OR old-fashioned	300 mL
	rolled oats	
½ cup	firmly packed brown sugar	125 mL
½ tsp.	cinnamon	2 mL
¼ cup	butter	50 mL

Prepare base by sprinkling lemon juice over blueberries. Combine sugar and flour. Add to the blueberries, tossing with a fork to coat evenly. Place in an 8'' (2 L) square baking dish. Combine all topping ingredients, mixing until crumbly. Sprinkle over the fruit base. Bake at 375°F (190°C) for 25-30 minutes. **Serving Suggestion:** Serve warm with ice cream. **Serves:** 4-6.

Mrs. Helen MacPhail
Wife of the Lieutenant-Governor of Prince Edward Island

Holly Wreath Fish Bake

6.5 oz.	can, lobster	185 g
6.5 oz.	can, crab	185 g
4 oz.	can, shrimp	113 g
6.5 oz.	can, tuna	185 g
1 cup	finely chopped celery	250 mL
2 tbsp.	finely chopped onion	25 mL
1½ cups	mayonnaise	375 mL
½ tsp.	salt	2 mL
½ tsp.	Worcestershire sauce	2 mL
1 cup	dry bread crumbs	250 mL
2 tbsp.	melted butter	25 mL

Drain cans of fish and break fish into chunks. Combine with remaining ingredients, except bread crumbs and melted butter, tossing lightly. Place in a greased 2-quart (2 L) baking dish. Add crumbs to butter, then spread over top of mixture. Bake at 350°F (180°C) for 30 minutes. **Serves:** 8 generously.

Hon. Muriel McQ. Fergusson
New Brunswick

My Favorite Casserole

2 x 10 oz.	cans, cream of mushroom soup	2 x 284 mL
½ cup	cold water	125 mL
2 cups	cooked, diced chicken	500 mL
2 cups	diced celery	500 mL
1 cup	diced onion	250 mL
1 cup	diced green pepper	250 mL
½ lb.	can, cashew nuts	250 g
2 x 2¾ oz.	cans, toasted chinese noodles	2 x 78 g

Place soup in a 2-quart (2 L) baking dish. Add water and stir until smooth. Add chicken, celery, onion, green pepper, nuts and 1 can of noodles. Mix lightly. Sprinkle remaining can of noodles over top. Bake at 350°F (180°C) for 1 hour. **Serves:** 8.

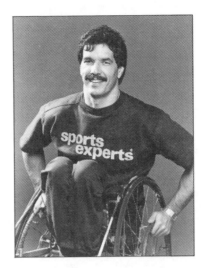

Andre Viger
Quebec Athlete

Rhubarb Crisp

4 cups	diced rhubarb	1 L
1 cup	sugar	250 mL
¼ cup	flour	50 mL
½ tsp.	cinnamon	2 mL
½ cup	water	125 mL
1 cup	flour	250 mL
½ cup	quick-cooking rolled oats	125 mL
1 cup	packed brown sugar	250 mL
½ cup	melted butter	125 mL
	cream	

Combine rhubarb, sugar, flour and cinnamon. Turn into a buttered 8" (2 L) baking dish. Pour water over all. In a bowl, combine flour, rolled oats, brown sugar and melted butter, mixing with a fork to form a crumbly mixture. Sprinkle over rhubarb mixture. Bake at 375°F (190°C) for 35 minutes or until rhubarb is tender. Serve warm with cream. **Serves:** 6.

Hon. Jack Riddell
Ontario Minister of Agriculture and Food

Brown Betty Pudding

8	medium Ontario apples, about 2 lbs. (1 kg)	8
½ cup	water	125 mL
¼ cup	sugar	50 mL
½ tsp.	cinnamon	2 mL
½ tsp.	vanilla	2 mL
pinch	salt	pinch
½ cup	packed brown sugar	125 mL
¾ cup	flour	175 mL
¼ tsp.	freshly grated nutmeg	1 mL
½ tsp.	cinnamon	2 mL
⅓ cup	butter	75 mL

Peel, core and thinly slice apples. Place in a buttered 8" (2 L) baking dish. In a small bowl, combine the water, sugar, first ½ tsp. (2 mL) cinnamon, vanilla and salt. Pour over apples and toss to coat. In a small bowl, stir together the brown sugar, flour, nutmeg and second ½ tsp. (2 mL) cinnamon. Cut in butter. Spread mixture over apples. Bake at 375°F (190°C) for 30-40 minutes or until apples are tender and top is browned. **Serving Suggestion:** Serve warm with cheese, whipped cream or vanilla ice cream. **Serves:** 4-6.

Pearl McGonigal
Manitoba Lieutenant-Governor, 1981-86

Sensational Roast Pork

5 lb.	pork loin roast*	2.5 kg
14 oz.	can, unsweetened cherries with juice	398 mL
¼ cup	brown sugar	50 mL
¼ tsp.	dry mustard	1 mL
½ tsp.	salt	2 mL
1	garlic clove, minced	1
2 tsp.	flour	10 mL
3 tbsp.	vinegar	50 mL

*Have the butcher bone and retie roast — this makes it easier to carve. Place meat, fat side up, in a roasting pan. Drain cherries, reserving juice, and set cherries aside. Combine cherry juice, brown sugar, mustard, salt, garlic, flour and vinegar, mixing until smooth. Pour over meat. Bake at 325°F (160°C), 30-35 minutes per pound (500 g). Baste every 20 minutes during roasting. Add reserved cherries during last 30 minutes to heat thoroughly. Let roast rest for 15 minutes before serving. Serve cherry sauce with meat. **Serves:** 6-8.

Premier Grant Devine
Premier of Saskatchewan

Chinese Hamburger Casserole

1 lb.	ground beef	500 g
2 cups	diagonally sliced celery	500 mL
10 oz.	pkg., frozen peas, thawed	283 g
¾ cup	chopped onion	175 mL
10 oz.	can, cream of mushroom soup	284 mL
2 tbsp.	milk	25 mL
2 tbsp.	soy sauce	25 mL
½ tsp.	pepper	2 mL
1 cup	crushed potato chips paprika	250 mL

Brown ground beef in a frying pan and place in bottom of a 2-quart (2 L) baking dish. Place celery on top of meat, then layer with peas. Combine onion, soup, milk, soy sauce and pepper to make a sauce. Pour sauce over peas and top with crushed potato chips. Sprinkle with paprika. Bake at 375°F (190°C) for 30 minutes. **Serves:** 6.

Wayne Gretzky
Alberta Athlete

Chili à la Wayne

This delicious recipe is perfect for impromptu gatherings. No measuring is required — it depends on how many people and what your tastes are!

1-1½ lbs.	ground beef	500-750 g
5½ oz.	can, tomato paste	156 mL
19 oz.	can, tomatoes	540 mL
14 oz.	can, kidney beans	398 mL
2 x 14 oz.	cans, brown beans	2 x 398 mL
	red wine to taste	
	carrots, broccoli, cauliflower, celery and green peppers, sliced, your choice	
	Tabasco sauce to taste	
	Worcestershire sauce to taste	
	salt and pepper to taste	
14 oz.	can, pineapple chunks	398 mL

Brown ground beef. Add all other ingredients, stirring to combine. Cover and simmer for at least 1 hour. The longer it cooks, the thicker and tastier it will become. **Serves:** 8-10 or more.

Rick Hansen
British Columbia Athlete

Survival Spaghetti Sauce

Recipe supplied by "Tour Cook" Mike Reid.

7½ cups	canned tomatoes	1.875 L
21 oz.	can tomato sauce	596 mL
2 x 13 oz.	cans tomato paste	2 x 369 mL
2 tsp.	lemon pepper	10 mL
3 tsp.	Italian seasoning	15 mL
3 tsp.	oregano	15 mL
1 tsp.	thyme	5 mL
3	large green peppers, cubed	3
2	large red peppers, cubed	2
3	medium zucchini, cubed	3
5 cups	sliced mushrooms	1.25 L
4 lbs.	ground beef	2 kg
2	large onions, diced	2

Mix tomatoes, tomato sauce and tomato paste in a large saucepan over low heat. Add seasonings and vegetables to sauce. Brown ground beef in a frying pan. Add onions and sauté until transparent, then add to sauce. Simmer for 2 hours, stirring occasionally. **Serves:** 24 or more.

Federated Women's Institutes of Canada

An inscription under a portrait in the Canadian Agricultural Hall of Fame reads:

Mrs. Adelaide Hoodless 1857-1910

Although her sphere of activity was confined to Canada, the name has become known around the world. She was the driving force behind the founding of the Women's Institutes, an organization which is worldwide in scope. Because of her efforts, women in all parts of the world have an opportunity to become better homemakers and more effective community leaders. Early in her career, she was instrumental in establishing cooking classes for public school girls at the Hamilton YWCA. Later she persuaded the Ontario Government to initiate domestic science courses at the Ontario Normal School. Due to her influence, Sir William Macdonald agreed to provide funds for the establishment of the college which bears his name, for the teaching of Agriculture and Domestic Science. In addition to these achievements and many others, she assisted in organizing the National Council of Women and the Victorian Order of Nurses.

"Nominated by the Federated Women's Institute of Ontario".

Inspired by a personal tragedy, the death of her 18-month-old son from con-taminated milk, Adelaide Hoodless determined to work for the education of women and the welfare of the family. In 1897, at Stoney Creek, Ontario she founded a Women's Institute to further these goals. By 1915 all Canadian provinces had a W.I. organization. During the war each province devoted their time to patriotic endeavors. When the war ended in 1918, the Institutes started thinking about new activities and uppermost in their thoughts was the idea that the time had come for some national link binding them all together.

A meeting was called for February 1919 in Winnipeg and at this meeting, twenty-two years after meeting in Stoney Creek, the Federated Women's Institutes of Canada became a National Organization with the approval of the Federal Minister of Agriculture. At this time a Western newspaper stated, "In the Federation of Women's Institutes, there has arisen a mighty force whose influence knows no bounds."

The aims and objects of the national federation are, briefly,

1) to coordinate provincial units through a system of conveners, national, provincial and local
2) to raise the standard of homemaking
3) to act as a clearing house for activities of the provincial organizations
4) to develop agriculture to meet the food needs of the human race
5) to promote educational, moral, social and economic measures according to the objects of the Federation
6) to encourage cooperation in community efforts
7) to initiate nationwide campaigns according to the objects of the federation.

Today there are over 40,000 F.W.I.C. members and more than 2,000 branches across Canada, with a national office in Ottawa. F.W.I.C. is always helping those less fortunate, be it at home or in other parts of the world. Projects have ranged from submissions on Pensions, Aging, Status of Women, Divorce Reform and Mechanisms for Youth Training, to Nutrition Studies, assistance to 4-H Groups and raising funds for projects in Third-World countries, including water wells for Kenya and Zambia.

As a former president of A.C.W.W., a worldwide organization of which F.W.I.C. is a constituent member, said, "The Story of Stoney Creek has four important and significant points for us to remember. First, it shows the power of an idea — and can be more powerful than armies; second it shows the power of a woman; third, it shows the power of an individual; and fourth, it proves that everyone must begin where they are with what they have".

Federated Women's Institutes of Canada

F.W.I.C. Policy:

F.W.I.C. is strictly nonpartisan, nonsectarian and nonracial in every phase of its work.

F.W.I.C. is a consituent society of the Associated Country Women of the World which is a worldwide organization of nine million (9,000,000) rural women.

F.W.I.C. Committees:

Educational

1. Agriculture
2. Canadian Industries
3. Citizenship and Legislation
4. Education and Cultural Activities
5. Home Economics and Health
6. International Affairs

Special

1. Safety
2. Northern Canada Women's Institute
3. Canadian Unity
4. Federated News

F.W.I.C. Membership:

Consists of Women's Institutes of Alberta, British Columbia, Manitoba, New Brunswick, Newfoundland and Labrador, Nova Scotia, Ontario, P.E.I., Quebec and Saskatchewan.

F.W.I.C. Women Are:

Educators
Homemakers
Nurses
Farmers
Bus Drivers

Secretaries
Politicians
Clerks
Volunteers
and more

Concerns of F.W.I.C.:

Agricultural Economy
Equality for Women
Human Rights
Status for Homemakers
Child Care
Pensions
Pornography

Divorce Law Reform
Child Abuse
Family Violence
Health Services
Effect of Technology on Women
Environment
Canadian Unity

Historical Highlights:

1897 — first Women's Institute organized at Stoney Creek, Ontario.

1919 — Federated Women's Institutes of Canada formed.

1929 — F.W.I.C. first national organization to have a share in International Peace Garden.

1933 — the Associated Country Women of the World formed.

1945 — Lady Tweedsmuir presented three cups for a Triennial Competition in Community History, Cultural Competition and Handicrafts.

1957 — Senator Cairine Wilson presented silver bowl for Triennial Competition in Citizenship.

1957 — first National Convention held in Ottawa.

1958 — national office established in Ottawa.

1959 — F.W.I.C. bought Adelaide Hunter Hoodless Homestead.

1982 — Past President's Essay Competition inaugurated for children under the age of 14.

1986 — Established International Development Fund.

1988 — Published "Cooking Collections" cookbook.

The Associated Country Women of the World

The Associated Country Women of the World is the only international organization of country women and homemakers. Its multi-million members live in more than 70 countries in all five continents.

A.C.W.W. is nonparty political, nonsectarian and nonracial. It is open to all members of organized bodies of country women and homemakers, or associations of women which include a substantial number of country members, having power to elect their own officers and to lay down their own policy, and whose aims are in harmony with those of A.C.W.W.

Societies are autonomous in their own work but are linked together (whether Constituent, Associate or Corresponding Societies) to form A.C.W.W. as their international organization. Individual nonvoting membership is also available.

Aims
— To raise the standard of living of women everywhere and their families.
— To promote international goodwill, friendship and understanding between country women and homemakers everywhere.
— To work together for relief of poverty and to promote the advancement of education, the relief of sickness and the preservation of health.
— To be a forum for country women and homemakers on international affairs, speaking with an informed voice for them in the Councils of the World.
— **Activities**

  To promote interest and work together for the betterment of both rural and urban families and communities through study and action in the spheres of homemaking, housing, health and hygiene, education, the principals of good citizenship, all aspects of agriculture, including the production, distribution and use of food, in order to achieve the basic necessities for healthier and better living conditions.

What A.C.W.W. Does
— Works for IMPROVED STANDARDS OF LIVING for women and families.
— Supports PROJECTS organized locally by members to promote basic education to fight hunger and disease.
— Trains local women for LEADERSHIP in developing countries, through courses, seminars and individual scholarships (Lady Aberdeen and Elsie Zimmern Scholarship and Nutrition Education Schemes).
— Speak for its members and airs their problems at the UNITED NATIONS where it has consultative status. It also gives to members firsthand information about the U.N. and its specialized agencies.
— Encourages new local societies for country women and homemakers.
— Holds a world conference (THE TRIENNIAL CONFERENCE) every three years. Every society may be represented and also individual members.
— Arranges REGIONAL CONFERENCES through its Area Presidents.
— Puts members IN TOUCH through Letter and Exchange Programs.

Ontario

The Fruit Belt

Ontario is blessed with an abundance of agricultural products but nothing symbolizes the harvest more than the lush colors of the province's orchards and vineyards. Apples, apricots, cherries, grapes, peaches, pears and plums create a cornucopia of colors and flavors that will explode in the next pages as you read the recipes of our Ontario cooks.

Of all the fruits grown in Ontario, one of the most well-known is the McIntosh apple. The McIntosh was discovered in 1811 by John McIntosh of Dundas County, Ontario. It wasn't exactly an instant success story, though. One tree in Mr. McIntosh's orchard produced fragrant red apples with a juicy white flesh, a crisp texture and the distinctive, moderately tart flavor we have come to know and love. But, although Mr. McIntosh sold seedlings from these apples, none of the trees that grew from them bore the same fruit as the original.

The world had to wait until 1835 when John McIntosh's son, Allen, successfully reproduced the species through grafting and budding techniques. From this start, the McIntosh spread across the country and around the world.

Many of the other apple varieties we now use regularly have been produced by cross-breeding using the McIntosh. These include the Cortland, Melba, Maroun, Spartan and others.

The original tree that produced the first McIntosh apples flourished until 1894, when it died after being badly damaged by fire.

So, whether apples are your favorite or you prefer any of the other varieties of tree fruit, you're sure to find a recipe to suit your tastes from "The Fruit Belt" of Ontario.

Ginger-Pear Crumble, page 112

Ontario Corn Bread

1 cup	milk	250 mL
¼ cup	sugar	50 mL
1 tbsp.	salt	15 mL
¼ cup	shortening	50 mL
¾ cup	water	175 mL
1 cup	cornmeal	250 mL
1 tsp.	sugar	5 mL
½ cup	lukewarm water	125 mL
1 tbsp.	active dry yeast (1 pkg.)	15 mL
6-6½ cups	flour	1.5-1.625 L

Scald milk and pour into a large bowl. Add ¼ cup (50 mL) sugar, salt, shortening, water and cornmeal. Stir until shortening melts. Meanwhile, dissolve 1 tsp. (5 mL) sugar in lukewarm water. Over this sprinkle the yeast. Let stand for 10 minutes, then stir briskly with a fork. Add softened yeast to milk mixture and stir. Beat in 3 cups (750 mL) flour. Add another 3-3½ cups (750-875 mL) flour as necessary. Work in last of flour by hand. Turn dough out onto a lightly floured surface and knead for 8-10 minutes. Shape into smooth ball and place in a greased bowl, rotating dough to grease surface. Cover and let rise until doubled, about 1½ hours. Punch down and shape into 2 loaves. Place in 2, 9 x 5" (2 L) loaf pans that have been greased and sprinkled with cornmeal. Grease tops of loaves and let rise again until doubled, about 1¼ hours. Bake at 425°F (220°C) for 30 minutes. **Yield:** 2 loaves.

Peach Pie

1	9" (23 cm) unbaked pastry shell	1
⅓ cup	flour	75 mL
½ cup	sugar	125 mL
1 cup	sour cream	250 mL
5 cups	quartered, peeled peaches, about 9	1.25 L
¼ cup	lightly packed brown sugar	50 mL

Line pie plate with pastry. Trim, flute edge, but do not prick. Combine flour, sugar and sour cream and beat with an electric beater until smooth. Arrange peaches, flat edge down, in concentric circles in pastry shell. Pour sour cream mixture over peaches. Bake at 450°F (230°C) for 15 minutes. Reduce heat to 350°F (180°C) and bake for an additional 30-35 minutes or until filling is set. Sprinkle brown sugar over the pie. Broil for 2-3 minutes or until sugar is melted. Serve warm. **Serves:** 6. See photograph on front cover.

Apple Oatmeal Squares

1 cup	flour	250 mL
1 cup	quick-cooking rolled oats	250 mL
½ cup	firmly packed brown sugar	125 mL
1 tsp.	nutmeg	5 mL
½ tsp.	salt	2 mL
¾ cup	butter	175 mL
6	medium apples	6
¼ cup	sunflower seeds	50 mL

Combine flour, rolled oats, sugar, nutmeg and salt. Cut in butter until mixture is crumbly. Measure out ½ cup (125 mL) and set aside for topping. Press remaining mixture evenly into the bottom of a greased 9" (2.5 L) square baking dish. Peel and core apples. Cut in halves lengthwise. Place cut side down on oatmeal base. Add sunflower seeds to reserved topping mixture and sprinkle over apples. Bake at 375°F (190°C) for 40-45 minutes. Cut in squares and serve warm or cold. **Yield:** 12 squares.

Apple Waldorf Salad

2½ cups	diced apples	625 mL
2 tsp.	lemon juice	10 mL
	boiling water	
¼ cup	raisins, washed	50 mL
⅓ cup	diced celery	75 mL
⅓ cup	walnuts (optional)	75 mL
pinch	salt	pinch
dash	white pepper	dash
¼ cup	mayonnaise OR salad dressing	50 mL
1 tsp.	chopped parsley (optional)	5 mL

Sprinkle apples with lemon juice. Pour boiling water over raisins; set aside for 5 minutes. Drain well and add to apples. Add remaining ingredients, tossing lightly. Refrigerate 1-2 hours before serving. **Serves:** 6.

Cheese-Baked Apples

3 tbsp.	sugar	50 mL
2 tbsp.	brown sugar	25 mL
2 tbsp.	flour	25 mL
¾ tsp.	cinnamon	3 mL
¼ tsp.	salt	1 mL
⅓ cup	water	75 mL
1 tbsp.	lemon juice	15 mL
6	medium apples, peeled, cored and cut into 8 slices each	6
½ cup	shredded Cheddar cheese	125 mL

Combine sugars, flour, cinnamon and salt. Stir in water and lemon juice. Add apple slices, stirring to coat. Arrange apple slices in a 9" (23 cm) pie plate. Drizzle sugar mixture over all. Bake, covered, at 350°F (180°C) for 45-50 minutes or until apples are tender. Uncover and sprinkle with cheese. Bake, uncovered, for 5 additional minutes. **Serves:** 6.

Jellied Apple Snow

3 oz.	pkg., red gelatin	85 g
2 cups	hot water	500 mL
1	egg white	1
1 tsp.	lemon juice	5 mL
1 cup	applesauce	250 mL
	red and green cherries for garnish	

Dissolve gelatin in hot water. When gelatin is slightly thickened, beat until frothy. In a separate bowl, beat egg white until stiff. Beat lemon juice and applesauce into whipped gelatin, then fold in egg white. Decorate with red and green cherries. Chill 4 hours or longer before serving. **Serves:** 4-6.

Apricot Jam

2 qts.	ripe apricots	2 L
¼ cup	lemon juice	50 mL
7½ cups	sugar	1.875 L
1	bottle liquid fruit pectin	1

Prepare fruit - peel, pit and chop very finely. Measure 4 cups (1 L) prepared fruit into a large saucepan. Add lemon juice. Add the exact amount of sugar, mixing well. Place over high heat and bring to a full rolling boil. Boil hard for 1 minute, stirring constantly. Remove from heat. Immediately stir in pectin. Stir 3-5 minutes. Skim off foam using a metal spoon. Pour quickly into sterilized jars and seal. **Yield:** 8 cups (2 L).

Cherry Pudding

¾ cup	cherry pie filling	175 mL
3 tbsp.	softened butter	50 mL
⅓ cup	sugar	75 mL
1	egg	1
½ tsp.	vanilla	2 mL
1 cup	pastry flour	250 mL
1½ tsp.	baking powder	7 mL
dash	salt	dash
½ cup	milk	125 mL

Grease top part of a 1½-quart (1.5 L) double boiler. Pour in cherry pie filling. In a bowl, cream butter. Add sugar and mix until creamy. Beat in egg and vanilla. In a separate bowl, combine flour, baking powder and salt. Add dry ingredients alternately with milk to creamed mixture. Pour batter over cherry pie filling. Cover tightly and place over boiling water in double boiler. Cook about 2 hours or until firm. **Serves:** 4.

Luscious Cherry Pie

	pastry for 9" (23 cm) double-crust pie	
2 cups	pitted cherries	500 mL
⅓ cup	cherry juice	75 mL
¼ tsp.	almond extract	1 mL
⅓ cup	sugar	75 mL
⅓ cup	brown sugar	75 mL
3 tbsp.	quick-cooking tapioca	50 mL
1 tbsp.	butter	15 mL

Prepare pastry. Combine cherries, juice, almond extract, sugars and tapioca. Let stand for 15 minutes. Pour into pastry-lined pie plate. Dot with butter. Adjust top pastry crust and flute and trim edge. Bake at 450°F (230°C) for 10 minutes. Reduce heat to 350°F (180°C) and bake for an additional 30 minutes. **Serves:** 6.

Grape Pie

1	9" (23 cm) unbaked pastry shell	1
5 cups	washed and stemmed Ontario grapes	1.25 L
1 cup	sugar	250 mL
2 tbsp.	cornstarch	25 mL
¼ tsp.	salt	1 mL
2 tsp.	lemon juice	10 mL
⅓ cup	flour	75 mL
2 tbsp.	sugar	25 mL
2 tbsp.	butter	25 mL

Prepare pastry. Prepare filling by slipping skins off grapes, reserve. Place pulp in a saucepan and bring to a boil. Reduce heat. Simmer for 5 minutes. Sieve and remove seeds. Mix sugar, cornstarch, salt and lemon juice. Add sugar mixture and skins to grape pulp; stir to combine. Pour filling into pastry shell. Prepare topping by combining the flour and sugar. Cut in butter until crumbly. Sprinkle topping over filling in pastry shell. Bake at 425°F (220°C) for 30 minutes. Chill before serving to allow filling to thicken. **Serves:** 6.

Orange Tart Shells

2 cups	flour	500 mL
1 tsp.	salt	5 mL
¾ cup	shortening	175 mL
1 tbsp.	grated orange rind	15 mL
5 tbsp.	orange juice	75 mL

Combine flour and salt. Cut in shortening until mixture resembles coarse meal. Add orange rind. Stirring with a fork, add orange juice, 1 tbsp. (15 mL) at a time, to flour mixture to make dough hold together. Press into a ball. Chill dough and roll out. Place into tart pans and prick with a fork. Bake at 425°F (220°C) for about 10 minutes or until slightly brown. Use in Plum Elegant Tarts (see recipe, page 114) or fill with filling of your choice.

Banana Peach Jam

1 cup	mashed ripe bananas	250 mL
3¼ cups	peeled and mashed ripe Ontario peaches	800 mL
½ cup	chopped maraschino cherries, well drained	125 mL
2 tbsp.	lemon juice	25 mL
2 oz.	pkg. powdered fruit pectin	57 g
6 cups	sugar	1.5 L

Combine bananas, peaches, cherries and lemon juice in a very large saucepan or preserving kettle. Add powdered pectin and mix well. Place over heat and stir fruit mixture until it comes to a full boil. Immediately stir in sugar. Return to a full rolling boil. Boil and stir for 1 minute. Remove from heat and skim off foam, using a metal spoon. Stir and skim by turns for 5 minutes, to cool slightly and prevent floating fruit. Pour quickly into hot sterilized jars. Seal. Store in a cool, dry place. **Yield:** 6 cups (1.5 L).

Peach Dessert

28 oz.	can, sliced peaches and juice	796 mL
19 oz.	pkg., butter pecan cake mix	520 g
1 cup	pecan halves	250 mL
1 cup	shredded coconut	250 mL
½ cup	melted butter	125 mL

Cover bottom of a 9 x 13'' (4 L) baking dish with peaches and juice. Sprinkle dry cake mix over top. Sprinkle nuts and coconut evenly over cake mix, then drizzle melted butter over top. Bake at 325°F (160°C) for 55-60 minutes. **Serves:** 12.

Old-Fashioned Pear Jam

6 cups	peeled and mashed pears	1.5 L
4 cups	brown sugar	1 L

Place mashed pears in crock or glass bowl and add brown sugar. Let stand, refrigerated, overnight. Put in cooking pot and boil down to the consistency of applesauce. Pour into sterilized jars and seal. **Yield:** 6 cups (1.5 L).

Ginger-Pear Crumble

1½ cups	gingersnap cookie crumbs	375 mL
¼ cup	melted butter	50 mL
3½ cups	pear halves and juice	875 mL
1 tbsp.	lemon juice	15 mL
½ cup	brown sugar	125 mL
½ tsp.	salt	2 mL
½ tsp.	cinnamon	2 mL
¼ tsp.	nutmeg	1 mL

Mix crumbs and butter. Put ½ of crumb mixture in the bottom of a 9" (2.5 L) square baking dish. Place pear halves on the crumb base. Measure ¼ cup (50 mL) pear juice and add lemon juice. Sprinkle over pears. Combine sugar, salt and spices and spread over top. Cover with remaining crumb mixture. Bake at 350°F (180°C) for 25 minutes. **Serves:** 8. See photograph on page 104A.

Pear Crumb Pie

1	9" (23 cm) unbaked pastry shell	1
4 cups	sliced pears	1 L
2 tbsp.	lemon juice	25 mL
⅔ cup	sugar	150 mL
1½ tbsp.	quick-cooking tapioca	22 mL
½ cup	flour	125 mL
½ cup	brown sugar	125 mL
¼ tsp.	cinnamon	1 mL
¼ cup	butter	50 mL

Prepare pastry. Combine pears, lemon juice, sugar and tapioca. Mix all together and turn into pastry-lined pie plate. Prepare topping by combining flour, brown sugar and cinnamon. Cut in butter until crumbly. Sprinkle crumbs on top of pears. Bake at 400°F (200°C) for 10 minutes. Reduce heat to 350°F (180°C) and bake until nicely browned, about 40-50 minutes longer. **Serves:** 6.

Stuffed Pears

4	pears	4
½ cup	blanched, chopped almonds	125 mL
12	dates	12
¼ cup	sugar	50 mL
½ cup	water	125 mL

Peel, core and halve pears. Fill centers with almonds. Place a date in the center of each pear half. Place pears in a baking dish. Combine sugar, water and remaining dates. Pour over pears. Bake at 350°F (180°C) for about 30 minutes or until pears are tender. Baste several times with the syrup. Take care not to break pears while cooking. **Serves:** 4.

Plum Chutney

3 lbs.	prune plums, about 24-30	1.5 kg
1 lb.	green apples, 3 medium	500 g
1	large onion	1
2-4 tsp.	finely chopped preserved ginger OR ½-1 tsp. (2-5 mL) ground ginger	10-20 mL
¼ tsp.	cayenne pepper	1 mL
1 tbsp.	mixed pickling spice	15 mL
2 cups	vinegar	500 mL
2 cups	sugar	500 mL
2 tsp.	salt	10 mL

Pit plums and chop into pieces. Peel and chop apples and onion. Tie spices in a cheesecloth bag. Place fruit and spice bag in a preserving kettle and add vinegar, sugar and salt. Stir well to combine. Simmer until tender and chutney is of proper consistency, about 2-2½ hours. Remove spice bag. Pour into sterilized jars and seal. **Yield:** Approximately 5 cups (1.25 L).

Plum Elegant Tarts

	baked Orange Tart Shells (see recipe, page 110)	
24	plums	24
½ cup	water	125 mL
1 cup	sugar	250 mL
1 tbsp.	cornstarch	15 mL
1 tbsp.	water	15 mL

Prepare tart shells. Remove pits from plums, cutting each plum in 8 slices. Combine plums, water and sugar and cook until tender. Dissolve cornstarch in water and add to plum mixture. Cook until thick and clear. Cool to lukewarm and pour into baked tart shells.

Fresh Plum Pie

	pastry for 9" (23 cm) double-crust pie	
16-18	ripe prune plums	16-18
½ cup	brown sugar	125 mL
½ cup	sugar	125 mL
dash	salt	dash
¼ tsp.	nutmeg	1 mL
pinch	ground cloves	pinch
2 tbsp.	quick-cooking tapioca	25 mL
1½ tsp.	lemon juice	7 mL
1 tbsp.	butter	15 mL

Prepare pastry. Cut plums into quarters, removing pits. Combine sugars, salt, nutmeg, cloves and tapioca. Add to fruit. Turn fruit mixture into pastry-lined pie plate. Sprinkle with lemon juice and dot with butter. Cover with top pastry crust, vent, trim and flute rim. Bake at 400°F (200°C) for 10-15 minutes. Reduce heat to 350°F (180°C) and bake until fruit is tender and crust is browned, about 40-50 minutes. **Serves:** 6.

Fresh Fruit Glazed Pie

1	9" (23 cm) baked pastry shell sliced fresh fruit of your choice	1

Glaze:

1 cup	sugar	250 mL
1 cup	water	250 mL
pinch	salt	pinch
2 tbsp.	cornstarch	25 mL
2 tbsp.	flavored gelatin (same flavor as fruit used)	25 mL

Prepare pastry shell, then line with sliced fruit. Make glaze by combining sugar, water, salt and cornstarch in a heavy saucepan or double-boiler and cook until clear. Remove from heat and stir in gelatin. Pour glaze over fruit in pastry shell and let cool for 2-3 hours before serving. **Serving Suggestion:** Top with whipped cream or ice cream. **Serves:** 6.

Honeyed Fruit Kabobs

Fruit for each kabob:

4	wedges, unpeeled red apples	4
4	wedges, unpeeled pears	4
4	cubes, 1" (2.5 cm) each, cantaloupe	4
4	maraschino cherries	4

Honey Sauce:

½ cup	honey	125 mL
2 tbsp.	lemon juice	25 mL
2 tbsp.	butter	25 mL

Prepare fruit and set aside. Combine honey, lemon juice and butter in a small saucepan. Heat, stirring, until blended. Dip fruit pieces in honey sauce and thread alternately on skewers, leaving about 4" (10 cm) at each end for holding and propping. Barbecue 3-4" (7.5-10 cm) away from coals over very low fire until fruit is heated through, about 5 minutes. Brush occasionally with honey sauce and turn often during cooking to avoid scorching.

Manitoba

On Wing and Hoof

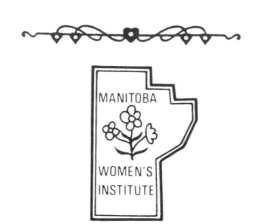

MANITOBA WOMEN'S INSTITUTE

"TO GOD IN HIS GLORY WE TWO NATIONS DEDICATE THIS GAR-
DEN AND PLEDGE OURSELVES THAT AS LONG AS MEN SHALL
LIVE, WE WILL NOT TAKE UP ARMS AGAINST ONE ANOTHER."

More than 50,000 people gathered on a hot, dry and dusty day, July 14th,
1932, to dedicate the International Peace Gardens straddling the Canada-
United States border between Boissevain, Manitoba and Dunseith, North
Dakota. North Dakota donated 888 acres, a mixture of farmland and forest.
Manitoba provided 1451 acres of forest reserve, rolling hills crowned with
paperbirch, oak, poplar and willow.

The Peace Gardens location is almost the exact center between the Atlantic
and Pacific oceans and is but 30 miles north of the exact center of the
North American continent. Manitoba Women's Institutes and the Federated Women's Institutes of Canada have adjacent picnic areas in the International Peace Gardens and these play host to thousands of visitors
each year. All are invited to enjoy the picnic area, the children's play area
and a general respite from the busy world.

Manitoba W. I. cooks also invite you to enjoy two of their unique foods —
wild rice and Winnipeg Goldeye. Wild rice traditionally accompanies game
and game birds and is a delicacy that has become better known in the
last two decades. The rice is a grain of an aquatic grass growing in marshes
of lakes in Eastern and Northern Manitoba and is harvested in the autumn.

Goldeye was first smoked by a Scotsman living in Winnipeg who became
lonely for his homeland and for the taste of his favorite fish — the kipper.
The fish that he smoked to a rosy hue is known today as Winnipeg Goldeye.

These traditional recipes will warm you up for the collection of poultry and
pork recipes to follow. Manitoba cooks up a storm "on wing and hoof"!

Chicken and Almonds in Sweet Sauce, page 122

Gourmet Wild Rice and Cheese Casserole

1 cup	Canadian wild rice	250 mL
¼ tsp.	salt	1 mL
3 cups	boiling water	750 mL
½ lb.	mushrooms, sliced	250 g
½ cup	chopped onion	125 mL
½ cup	butter	125 mL
1 cup	grated old Cheddar cheese	250 mL
19 oz.	can, tomatoes	540 mL
1 tsp.	salt	5 mL
1 cup	hot water	250 mL

Follow the quick-soak method (see below) to prepare wild rice for cooking. Cook rice, covered, in boiling salted water until nearly tender, about 30 minutes. Drain rice, if necessary. Sauté mushrooms and onion in butter for about 5 minutes. Toss rice with all other ingredients. Place in buttered 2-quart (2 L) baking dish. Cover and bake for 1 hour at 350°F (180°C). **Serves:** 8-10. See photograph on front cover.

Quick-soak Method of Preparing Wild Rice:

Wash required amount of wild rice under cold, flowing water. Stir rice into 3 times the amount of boiling water; 1 cup (250 mL) rice requires 3 cups (750 mL) water. Parboil for 5 minutes only. Remove from heat. Let soak in same water for 1 hour. Drain, wash and soak as directed in recipe. **Note:** 1 cup (250 mL) wild rice swells to about 4 times its size when cooked.

Winnipeg Goldeye

Goldeye may be cooked with head and tail on or off.

Method 1:

Place 1 Goldeye per serving on greased foil. Fold foil over fish, securing open edges with double folds to make package watertight. Place package in rapidly boiling water. When water returns to a boil, cover and cook 10 minutes (20 minutes if fish is frozen).

Method 2:

Unwrapped Goldeye may be cooked for 15-20 minutes in a steamer, or simmered in water for 10 minutes, or until fish flakes readily.

Method 3:

Place fish in a microwave-safe baking dish and cover with plastic wrap. Microwave on HIGH (full power) for 5½-8 minutes per pound (kg) or until fish flakes easily.

Chicken and Almonds in Sweet Sauce

4	chicken half-breasts, skinned and boned	4
2 tbsp.	vegetable oil	25 mL
2 tbsp.	soy sauce	25 mL
3	medium carrots, thinly sliced	3
½ cup	blanched, slivered almonds	125 mL
1	green pepper, chopped	1
1½ tbsp.	brown sugar	22 mL
1 cup	shredded red cabbage	250 mL
1 tbsp.	cornstarch	15 mL
3 tbsp.	water	50 mL

Cut chicken into bite-size cubes. On high heat, heat oil in wok or large frying pan. Add chicken cubes and stir-fry for 2 minutes. Sprinkle with soy sauce. Turn heat to medium, add carrots and mix. Cover and cook for 2 minutes. Add nuts and peppers and stir-fry for 3-4 minutes. Add sugar, mixing to dissolve. Add cabbage and stir-fry for 1 minute. Dissolve cornstarch in water. Add to wok, stirring until sauce thickens and becomes clear. **Serves:** 4.

Curried Chicken Breasts

4-6	chicken breasts	4-6
4 tbsp.	butter	60 mL
1 tsp.	curry powder	5 mL
2 cups	sliced onions	500 mL
1½ cups	sliced mushrooms	375 mL
1 cup	cream	250 mL
dash	cayenne pepper	dash
1½ tsp.	salt	7 mL
1 tbsp.	lemon juice	15 mL

Heat butter in frying pan. Brown chicken in hot butter. Add curry powder, onions and mushrooms and mix. Add remaining ingredients and simmer until tender or transfer to baking dish, cover and bake at 350°F (180°C) for 30-60 minutes. **Serves:** 4-6.

Chicken Italiano

14 oz.	can, tomatoes	398 mL
½ tsp.	basil	2 mL
½ tsp.	tarragon	2 mL
½ tsp.	salt	2 mL
¼ tsp.	pepper	1 mL
2 tsp.	butter	10 mL
1	garlic clove, chopped	1
4	chicken breasts, skinned	4
2 tbsp.	chopped fresh parsley	25 mL
½ cup	shredded mozzarella cheese	125 mL

Pour tomatoes into a blender. Add seasonings. Purée until smooth. Melt butter in a large frying pan. Sauté garlic over medium heat for 1 minute. Add chicken breasts, turning once or twice, and cook until golden on both sides. Turn chicken, fleshy side down, and cover with puréed tomato mixture. Bring to a boil, then reduce heat and simmer for 15 minutes, until tender. Remove chicken and place fleshy side up in a baking dish. Stir parsley into tomato sauce and spoon over chicken. Sprinkle with cheese. Place under heated broiler for 1 minute or just until cheese melts. **Serves:** 4.

Slow-Cooker Chicken Cacciatore

1	frying chicken, approximately 3 lbs. (1.5 kg), cut up	1
3 tbsp.	shortening	50 mL
2	medium onions, thinly sliced	2
2	garlic cloves, minced (optional)	2
2 cups	stewed tomatoes	500 mL
7½ oz.	can, tomato sauce	213 mL
⅓ cup	minced green pepper	75 mL
1 tsp.	salt	5 mL
¼ tsp.	black pepper	1 mL
¼ tsp.	cayenne pepper	1 mL
1 tsp.	oregano	5 mL
½ tsp.	basil	2 mL
½ tsp.	celery salt	2 mL
1	bay leaf	1
¼ cup	Chianti wine	50 mL

Brown chicken pieces in shortening in a frying pan. Remove chicken and set aside. Layer onion slices in slow cooker. Put browned chicken on top of onion. Add remaining ingredients. Cover. Cook on low heat for 6-8 hours, or on high heat for 3-4 hours. Discard bay leaf. **Serving Suggestion:** Serve chicken pieces with sauce over buttered pasta. **Serves:** 6-8.

Manitoba Chicken Superb

3-4 lbs.	chicken	1.5-2 kg
1 cup	flour	250 mL
1 tsp.	salt	5 mL
1 tsp.	paprika	5 mL
½ cup	butter	125 mL
	paprika	

Manitoba Chicken Superb (Cont'd.)

Cut chicken into pieces. Combine flour, salt and paprika. Dredge chicken pieces in flour mixture. Heat butter in a heavy frying pan. Thoroughly brown chicken in hot butter. Transfer chicken to baking dish, arranging back pieces and neck on the bottom and more meaty pieces with skin on top. Pour any remaining butter from pan over chicken. Sprinkle generously with paprika. Bake, uncovered, at 325°F (160°C) for about 1 hour or until tender. Remove accumulated fat from dish. **Note:** This chicken has a nice crisp crust. If softer crust is desired, cover baking dish for last 15 minutes of baking. **Serves:** 4-5.

Oven-Baked Parmesan Chicken

¾ cup	dry bread crumbs	175 mL
3 tbsp.	grated Parmesan cheese	50 mL
3 tbsp.	sesame seeds	50 mL
1 tbsp.	flour	15 mL
1 tsp.	salt	5 mL
¼ tsp.	thyme OR oregano	1 mL
¼ cup	vegetable oil	50 mL
¼ cup	butter	50 mL
1	garlic clove, crushed OR chopped	1
1-2½ lbs.	chicken fryer pieces OR 2-3 lbs. (1-1.5 kg) thighs OR drumsticks	500-1000 g
2 tbsp.	chopped parsley (optional)	25 mL

Combine first 6 ingredients and set aside. Heat oil and butter together. Sauté garlic until golden brown, then remove from heat. Coat chicken pieces in oil and butter mixture, then roll in reserved crumb mixture. Place chicken in a shallow baking dish. Spoon remaining oil and butter mixture over each chicken piece. Bake at 350°F (180°C) for 50-60 minutes. Sprinkle with chopped parsley just before serving, if desired. **Serves:** 2-4.

Triumphant Old Hen

1	boiling fowl	1
½ cup	flour	125 mL
2 tsp.	salt	10 mL
dash	pepper	dash
dash	poultry seasoning	dash
½ tsp.	paprika	2 mL
	butter OR chicken fat	
4 cups	water	1 L

Cut fowl into serving pieces. Mix flour, salt, pepper, poultry seasoning and paprika in a paper bag. Place chicken pieces in bag, hold top tightly closed and shake vigorously to thoroughly coat chicken. Heat fat and brown chicken pieces. Add water and simmer for about 3 hours, or until tender. Add more water during cooking as needed. **Serves:** 4-6.

Deep-Dish Chicken Pie

2 tbsp.	chopped onion	25 mL
2 tbsp.	melted butter	25 mL
½ cup	peas	125 mL
1 cup	cooked, sliced carrots	250 mL
1½ cups	cooked, sliced potatoes	375 mL
3 cups	cooked, diced chicken	750 mL
¼ cup	flour	50 mL
1 tsp.	salt	5 mL
dash	pepper	dash
2 cups	chicken stock	500 mL
2 tbsp.	chopped parsley	25 mL
	biscuit dough to cover	

Sauté onion in butter. Place alternate layers of onion, peas, carrots, potatoes and chicken in a greased 3-quart (3 L) casserole. In a saucepan, combine flour, salt and pepper. Blend in chicken stock and simmer until thick. Pour over vegetables and chicken. Sprinkle parsley over top. Top with a single crust of biscuit dough or individual biscuits. Bake at 425°F (220°C) for 15-20 minutes, or until biscuits are browned and chicken mixture is bubbly. **Serves:** 6-8.

Delicious Hot Chicken Salad

4 cups	cooked, diced chicken	1 L
1 cup	grated sharp cheese	250 mL
3½ oz.	pkg., slivered almonds	100 g
2 cups	diced celery	500 mL
3½ oz.	pkg., potato chips, crushed	100 g
10 oz.	can, cream of mushroom soup	284 mL
½ cup	mayonnaise	125 mL
4	hard-cooked eggs, chopped	4

Combine all ingredients, reserving ½ of the potato chips for topping. Mix well. Pour into a large baking dish. Top with reserved potato chips. Bake at 350°F (180°C) for 25 minutes. **Serves:** 12.

Prairie Chicken Casserole

A most important game bird of Manitoba, the Prairie Chicken makes a special occasion dish of sufficient stature to merit serving it with another Manitoba delicacy, wild rice.

1	prairie chicken, breast and legs of	1
	salt	
	water	
1	onion, sliced	1
10 oz.	can, cream of mushroom soup	284 mL
5½ oz.	can, mushrooms pieces and liquid	156 mL

Wash prairie chicken pieces thoroughly. Soak in salted water, ½ tbsp. (7 mL) salt to 1 cup (250 mL) water, overnight. Rinse well with cold water. Place chicken pieces in baking dish. Combine onion, soup, mushrooms and liquid and pour over chicken. Add enough water to cover. Bake, covered, at 350°F (180°C) for 1½-2 hours. **Serves:** 3-4.

Butterfly Chops Mexicana

4	**butterfly pork chops**	**4**
2 tbsp.	**butter**	**25 mL**
½ cup	**chopped green pepper**	**125 mL**
¼ cup	**chopped celery**	**50 mL**
¼ cup	**chopped onion**	**50 mL**
14 oz.	**can, tomatoes**	**398 mL**
7 oz.	**can, kernel corn**	**199 mL**
1 tsp.	**salt**	**5 mL**
½ tsp.	**chili powder**	**2 mL**

In a frying pan, brown chops in butter. Transfer to a baking dish. To the frying pan, add green pepper, celery and onion, cooking until tender. Add tomatoes, corn, salt and chili powder. Simmer for 10 minutes. Pour over chops. Cover and bake at 325°F (160°C) for 45 minutes. Remove cover and bake another 20-30 minutes, or until tender. **Serving Suggestion:** Serve over fluffy rice with a crisp salad and corn chips. **Serves:** 4.

Pork Cacciatore

1½ lbs.	**pork tenderloin**	**750 g**
2 tbsp.	**butter**	**25 mL**
1	**onion, diced**	**1**
½ lb.	**mushrooms, sliced**	**250 g**
1	**garlic clove, minced**	**1**
⅔ cup	**white wine OR chicken broth**	**150 mL**
1 tsp.	**salt**	**5 mL**
¼ tsp.	**pepper**	**1 mL**
¼ tsp.	**thyme**	**1 mL**
¼ tsp.	**parsley flakes**	**1 mL**
14 oz.	**jar spaghetti sauce**	**398 mL**

Cut pork in ¾" (2 cm) slices and flatten with a meat mallet. Heat butter in a frying pan and sauté onion, mushrooms and garlic. Add meat and brown. Transfer meat and vegetables to a large baking dish. Combine the wine and seasonings and pour over meat. Cover. Bake at 325°F (160°C) for 40 minutes. Stir in spaghetti sauce. Cover and bake another 10 minutes. **Serving Suggestion:** Serve over pasta. **Serves:** 4-6.

Sweet and Sour Pork

1 lb.	pork shoulder, cut into ½" (1 cm) chops	500 g
2	eggs, beaten	2
¼ cup	flour	50 mL
¼ tsp.	pepper	1 mL
½ cup	vegetable oil	125 mL

Sauce:

1 tbsp.	vegetable oil	15 mL
1 cup	pineapple juice	250 mL
½ cup	sugar	125 mL
3 tbsp.	cornstarch	50 mL
3 tbsp.	vinegar	50 mL
1 tbsp.	soy sauce	15 mL
6 tbsp.	water	100 mL
	sliced celery, green pepper and pineapple chunks (optional)	

Cut shoulder chops into ½" (1 cm) cubes. Mix eggs, flour and pepper together to make a smooth batter. Heat vegetable oil. Dip meat cubes into batter and fry slowly in hot oil until lightly browned. Drain on paper towels. To make the sauce, heat oil and pineapple juice in a saucepan. In a bowl, combine sugar and cornstarch, then add vinegar, soy sauce and water. Add the sugar mixture to the saucepan. Cook, stirring, until thickened. Add browned meat and simmer, covered, for 1½ hours. If desired, add celery, green pepper and pineapple chunks for last 30 minutes of cooking. Serve with rice. **Note:** The meat can be browned several days ahead and frozen until added to the hot sauce. **Serves:** 4-6.

Pork Chop and Apple Casserole

1 cup	boiling water	250 mL
½ cup	seedless raisins	125 mL
6	large, OR 12 small, pork chops	6
2	onions, thinly sliced	2
5	tart apples, cored and quartered	5
1 cup	beef stock	250 mL
1 tbsp.	brown sugar	15 mL
1 tbsp.	chopped parsley	15 mL
	salt and pepper to taste	
dash	EACH nutmeg, thyme and ground cloves	dash
1 tbsp.	currant jelly	15 mL

Pour boiling water over the raisins and let stand for 10 minutes. Meanwhile, brown chops quickly on each side in a frying pan. Transfer chops to baking dish. Pour raisins over chops. Add sliced onions and quartered apples. Combine beef stock, sugar and seasonings and pour over chops. Cover and bake at 350°F (180°C) for 1¼ hours. Stir jelly into sauce. Serve in baking dish.
Serves: 6.

Pork Mushroom Casserole

4-6	¾" (2 cm) pork loin chops	4-6
	pepper and paprika to taste	
2 tbsp.	butter	25 mL
	salt to taste	
½ cup	chopped celery	125 mL
½ cup	chopped onion	125 mL
1 tbsp.	parsley flakes	15 mL
10 oz.	can, cream of mushroom soup	284 mL
10 oz.	can, mushroom pieces	284 mL
⅓ cup	water OR milk	75 mL

Season chops with pepper and paprika. Sauté in butter over low heat. Season with salt. Transfer chops to a baking dish. Combine celery, onion, parsley, soup, mushrooms and water. Pour over chops. Cover and bake at 350°F (180°C) for 30 minutes. Turn chops and bake an additional 30 minutes, or until meat is no longer pink. **Serves:** 4-6.

Scalloped Pork Chops

6-8	pork chops	6-8
1 tbsp.	mustard	15 mL
1 tbsp.	vegetable oil	15 mL
4-6	medium potatoes, peeled and thinly sliced	4-6
1	small onion, chopped	1
10 oz.	can, cream of celery soup	284 mL
1	soup can full of milk	1
1-2 tsp.	salt	5-10 mL
¼ tsp.	pepper	1 mL
½ tsp.	marjoram OR sage	2 mL

On each pork chop, spread a little mustard. Brown chops in oil. In a large baking dish, arrange chops, potatoes and onion in layers. Combine soup, milk and seasonings and pour over chops. Cover and bake at 350°F (180°C) for 1½-2 hours. **Serves:** 6-8.

Tourtière (Pork Pies)

	pastry for 3, double-crust 9"	
	(23 cm) pies	
5 lbs.	**lean ground pork**	**2.5 kg**
1 lb.	**lean ground beef**	**500 g**
1	**large onion, chopped**	**1**
1	**garlic clove, minced**	**1**
2 tsp.	**salt**	**10 mL**
½ tsp.	**thyme**	**2 mL**
½ tsp.	**sage**	**2 mL**
½ tsp.	**dry mustard**	**2 mL**
¾ tsp.	**ground cloves**	**3 mL**
2 tsp.	**cinnamon**	**10 mL**
½ tsp.	**M.S.G. (optional)**	**2 mL**
1 tsp.	**celery salt**	**5 mL**
½ cup	**fine bread crumbs**	**125 mL**

Prepare pastry and set aside. In a large saucepan, combine all ingredients, except spices and bread crumbs. Add enough water to just cover meat mixture. Bring to the boiling point, then reduce heat slightly and continue to cook for 30 minutes, or until excess water is reduced. Add spices and bread crumbs, mixing well. Turn mixture into pastry-lined pie plates and cover with top pastry. Cut a few slashes in top crust to vent steam. Bake at 450°F (230°C) for 10 minutes. Reduce heat to 350°F (180°C) and bake an additional 20 minutes, or until crust is golden. Let cool completely, then freeze pies. These pies are better after they have been frozen. To reheat, bake at 325°F (160°C) for 1 hour. **Yield:** 3 meat pies.

Savory Sausage Dish

2 lbs.	small pork sausage	1 kg
2	medium onions, chopped	2
10 oz.	can, tomato soup	284 mL
1	egg	1
1 cup	milk	250 mL
1 cup	flour	250 mL
2 tsp.	baking powder	10 mL
pinch	salt	pinch

Fry sausages until light brown. Arrange in a baking dish. Sauté onions until transparent. Place onions over sausage, then pour soup over both. Beat egg and add milk. Combine dry ingredients and add to liquid, mixing to form a batter. Pour batter over sausage mixture. Bake at 400°F (200°C) for 35 minutes. **Serves:** 6-8.

Oven-Barbecued Spareribs

4 lbs.	pork spareribs	2 kg
¾ cup	minced onion	175 mL
1 cup	ketchup	250 mL
1 cup	water	250 mL
1½ tsp.	mustard	7 mL
¼ cup	sugar	50 mL
dash	cayenne pepper	dash
1	bay leaf	1
1½ tsp.	Worcestershire sauce	7 mL

Cut spareribs in 3-rib pieces. Brown lightly and place in a roasting pan. Combine all remaining ingredients in a saucepan and bring to a boil. Boil for 10 minutes, stirring to prevent scorching. Pour ½ the sauce over the spareribs, reserving the remainder of the sauce. Bake, covered, at 350°F (180°C) for 1¾ hours. Uncover during last 15 minutes of baking, basting several times. Discard bay leaf. Serve accompanied by the reserved hot sauce. **Serves:** 6.

Sweet and Sour Spareribs

3 lbs.	spareribs, cut in 2" (5 cm) lengths	1.5 kg
1	egg, beaten	1
½ cup	flour	125 mL
	vegetable oil	

Sauce:

⅔ cup	ketchup	150 mL
2 tbsp.	cornstarch	25 mL
¼ cup	vinegar	50 mL
½ cup	brown sugar	125 mL
1 cup	water	250 mL

Dip spareribs in beaten egg, then in flour. Heat oil and brown ribs. Place ribs in a roasting pan. Prepare sauce by combining all ingredients, mixing well. Pour sauce over the ribs. Cover and bake at 350°F (180°C) for 1 hour.
Serves: 4-6.

Saskatchewan

The Golden Seed

Saskatchewan is a place of endless space where, in the summer, on the prairies, the rolling fields of grain seem to go on forever. Yet, driving north from the grain fields you'll also find a land of lakes and forests — and some of the best fishing in the world.

Saskatchewan became a province in 1905 and the pace of settlement increased rapidly. By the 1920's most of the province's southern agricultural land was already in production.

Settlers came from many parts of the world including Europe, the United States and Eastern Canada. They brought with them different ideas and different lifestyles. As people struggled to build new communities where none had existed before, they learned from one another and soon accepted new ways. As a result, within one generation, a distinctive Saskatchewan way of life began to appear.

That spirit of cooperation that was necessary for survival in the days of early settlement still exists today in this province. With a population of one million people, Saskatchewan has more cooperatives per capita than any other province in Canada.

With a land base of over 49 million cultivated acres, Saskatchewan can produce 641 million bushels of grain and is one of the largest food-producing areas of our country.

Most Canadians probably hear the word "grain" and think "wheat". While wheat is a very important grain crop, there are many others as well. The W. I. cooks of Saskatchewan have assembled a variety of recipes using grain products for your enjoyment. Try the traditional rice and lentil recipes and then move on to delicious breads, buns and other favorites that use "the golden seed".

Whole-Wheat and Honey Pancakes, page 147

Rice Casserole

2 cups	cold water	500 mL
½ tsp.	salt	2 mL
1 cup	uncooked rice	250 mL
1	egg, beaten	1
¾ cup	milk	175 mL
½ cup	cottage cheese	125 mL
¾ cup	grated Cheddar cheese	175 mL
½ cup	vegetable oil	125 mL
1	medium onion, finely chopped	1
1 tbsp.	dried parsley	15 mL
1 tsp.	basil	5 mL
1 tsp.	salt	5 mL
dash	pepper	dash

Bring the cold water and salt to a boil, add the rice, cover and cook over low heat until all water is absorbed, about 20 minutes. Combine cooked rice and all other ingredients, mixing well. Turn into a greased 2-quart (2 L) baking dish. Bake at 350°F (180°C) for 1 hour. **Serves:** 6.

Honey-Baked Lentils

1 lb.	lentils, about 2½ cups (625 mL)	500 g
1	small bay leaf	1
5 cups	water	1.25 L
2 tsp.	salt	10 mL
1 cup	water	250 mL
1 tsp.	dry mustard	5 mL
¼ tsp.	cinnamon	1 mL
1 tbsp.	soy sauce	15 mL
½ cup	chopped onion	125 mL
½ lb.	ground beef OR sausage meat, browned	250 g
4	bacon slices, cut in pieces	4
⅓ cup	honey	75 mL

In a large saucepan, combine lentils, bay leaf, water and salt. Bring to a boil, cover and simmer for 30 minutes. Set aside, but do not drain. Remove bay leaf. In a separate bowl, combine water, mustard, cinnamon, soy sauce, onion and beef, mixing well. Add this mixture to the lentils. Turn into a baking dish. Sprinkle bacon on top. Pour honey over all. Cover and bake at 350°F (180°C) for 1 hour. Remove cover during last 10 minutes to brown bacon. **Serves:** 8-10.

Golden Sponge Cake

8	eggs, separated	8
1 cup	cold water	250 mL
2 cups	sugar	500 mL
2 cups	whole-wheat flour	500 mL
½ cup	cornstarch	125 mL
½ tsp.	salt	2 mL
1 tsp.	almond extract	5 mL
1 tsp.	cream of tartar	5 mL

Beat egg yolks until light colored. Add cold water and beat for 2 minutes. Add sugar gradually, beating until blended. In a separate bowl, combine flour, cornstarch and salt, mixing well. Add dry ingredients to egg yolk mixture, beating for 3-4 minutes. Add almond extract. Beat egg whites and cream of tartar until very stiff. Fold into batter. Pour batter into a tube cake pan and bake at 325°F (160°C) for 1¼ hours. Invert cake pan funnel on a glass to cool. **Serves:** 8-10.

Rolled-Oat Cake

1 cup	rolled oats	250 mL
1½ cups	boiling water	375 mL
½ cup	butter	125 mL
1 cup	brown sugar	250 mL
1 tsp.	vanilla	5 mL
1 cup	flour	250 mL
1 tsp.	baking soda	5 mL
½ tsp.	salt	2 mL
1 cup	chopped dates	250 mL
½ cup	chopped walnuts	125 mL

Put rolled oats in a bowl and add boiling water. Let stand until cool. Cream butter and sugar. Beat in rolled oats and vanilla. Combine flour, baking soda and salt. Add dry ingredients to rolled oats mixture, along with dates and nuts. Beat, blending well. Bake in a 9" (2.5 L) square baking dish at 350°F (180°C) for 35 minutes. **Serves:** 8.

Whole-Wheat 2-Egg Cake

1 cup	sugar	250 mL
½ cup	butter	125 mL
1 tsp.	vanilla	5 mL
2	eggs	2
2 cups	whole-wheat flour	500 mL
3 tsp.	baking powder	15 mL
½ tsp.	salt	5 mL
½ cup	milk	125 mL
¼ cup	orange juice	50 mL
1 tbsp.	orange rind	15 mL
¾ cup	chocolate chips	175 mL
½ cup	raisins	125 mL

Cream together the sugar, butter and vanilla. Add eggs, 1 at a time, beating well after each addition. Combine flour, baking powder and salt. Separately, combine milk, orange juice and rind. Add dry and liquid ingredients alternately to creamed mixture, mixing well. Fold in chocolate chips and raisins, being careful not to overbeat. Turn batter into a greased and floured 8" (2 L) square baking dish. Bake at 350°F (180°C) for 45-50 minutes. This cake is best served fresh. **Serves:** 8.

Carrot-Nut Torte

6	eggs, separated	6
10 tbsp.	honey	150 mL
1 cup	grated carrot	250 mL
1 cup	chopped walnuts	250 mL
1 tsp.	cinnamon	5 mL
½ cup	whole-wheat flour	125 mL
¼ cup	soy flour	50 mL
2 tbsp.	rice flour	25 mL
2 tbsp.	wheat germ	25 mL

Beat egg yolks and honey until light and creamy. Add carrots, walnuts, cinnamon, flours and wheat germ, mixing well. Beat egg whites until stiff. Fold into batter. Pour into a greased 8" (2 L) baking dish. Bake at 350°F (180°C) for 45 minutes. **Yield:** 32 bars.

Wheat Salad

2 cups	wheat	500 mL
	water	
8 oz.	pkg., cream cheese	250 g
2 tbsp.	lemon juice	25 mL
3½ oz.	pkg., vanilla, pecan OR butterscotch instant pudding	100 g
14 oz.	can, crushed pineapple, well drained	398 mL
2 cups	frozen dessert topping	500 mL

Soak wheat in water overnight. Rinse with cold water then cook in small amount of water over low heat for about 6 hours. Drain. Rinse with cold water. Combine cream cheese, lemon juice, pudding and pineapple, mixing well. Add cooked wheat. Just before serving, add dessert topping. **Serves:** 8-10.

Coconut Cookies

1¼ cups	flour	300 mL
1 tsp.	baking powder	5 mL
1 tsp.	baking soda	5 ml
½ tsp.	salt	2 mL
½ cup	sugar	125 mL
½ cup	brown sugar	125 mL
½ cup	butter, softened	125 mL
1	egg, beaten	1
½ tsp.	almond OR vanilla extract	2 mL
1 cup	instant rolled oats	250 mL
1 cup	shredded coconut	250 mL

Combine flour, baking powder, baking soda and salt in a large bowl. Add sugars, butter, egg and flavoring. Beat until smooth, about 2 minutes. Fold in rolled oats and coconut. Shape into small balls. Place on a greased baking sheet. Bake at 350°F (180°C) for 12-15 minutes. **Yield:** 36 cookies.

Raisin-Oat Cookies

½ cup	butter	125 mL
1 cup	brown sugar	250 mL
1	egg	1
½ cup	peanut butter	125 mL
1 tsp.	vanilla	5 mL
¾ cup	whole-wheat flour	175 mL
¼ cup	wheat germ, toasted	50 mL
½ cup	skim milk powder	125 mL
¾ tsp.	salt	3 mL
¼ tsp.	baking powder	1 mL
1 cup	quick-cooking rolled oats	250 mL
¼ tsp.	baking soda	1 mL
1 cup	raisins	250 mL
	sesame seeds (optional)	

Cream butter and sugar. Add egg, peanut butter and vanilla and cream until light. Combine dry ingredients. Add dry ingredients to creamed mixture, mixing well. Add raisins. Drop by spoonfuls onto a greased baking sheet and flatten to form cookies 2'' (5 cm) in diameter. Sprinkle with sesame seeds, if desired. Bake at 375°F (190°C) for 10 minutes. Carefully remove to rack to cool. **Yield:** 40 cookies.

Oh-So-Good Cookies

½ cup	butter	125 mL
⅓ cup	brown sugar	75 mL
½ cup	sugar	125 mL
1	egg, beaten	1
1 tsp.	vanilla	5 mL
1 cup	whole-wheat flour	250 mL
1 cup	rolled oats	250 mL
½ tsp.	baking soda	2 mL
¼ tsp.	salt	1 mL
½ cup	chopped nuts	125 mL
½ cup	raisins	125 mL

Cream together the butter and sugars. Beat in egg and vanilla. In a separate bowl, combine flour, rolled oats, baking soda and salt. Add to the creamed mixture, mixing well. Fold in nuts and raisins. Drop by spoonfuls onto an ungreased baking sheet. Bake at 375°F (190°C) for 8-10 minutes. Carefully lift cookies from sheet and cool on racks. **Yield:** 30 cookies.

Granola Cereal

¼ cup	wheat germ	50 mL
3 cups	rolled oats	750 mL
¼ cup	natural bran	50 mL
½ cup	sunflower seeds	125 mL
¼ cup	sesame seeds	50 mL
¼ cup	skim milk powder	50 mL
¼ cup	vegetable oil	50 mL
½ cup	frozen orange juice concentrate	125 mL
½ cup	raisins	125 mL
¼ cup	shredded coconut	50 mL

Mix all ingredients, except raisins and coconut, together thoroughly so that dry ingredients are well coated with oil and juice. Spread evenly on a baking sheet. Bake at 300°F (150°C) for 40 minutes until crisp, stirring often to ensure even browning. After baking, add raisins and coconut. Store in a closed container. Use ½ cup (125 mL) per serving. **Serves:** 10.

Sesame Seed Crackers

1 cup	whole-wheat flour	250 mL
¾ cup	oat bran	175 mL
¼ cup	flour	50 mL
½ cup	sesame seeds	125 mL
1 tsp.	salt	5 mL
¼ cup	caraway seeds, sunflower seeds OR wheat germ	50 mL
½ cup	cold water	125 mL
¼ cup	vegetable oil	50 mL

Combine first 6 ingredients, mixing well. Combine the water and oil, then add them to the dry ingredients, mixing until moist and crumbly. Add more water, if necessary. Press into a large baking sheet. Level with a rolling pin, mark in squares and prick with a fork. Bake at 325°F (160°C) until crisp and brown. **Yield:** 30-40 crackers.

Lentil Chili

4 cups	water	1 L
1 cup	lentils	250 mL
1 lb.	ground beef OR pork	500 g
1 cup	chopped onions	250 mL
28 oz.	can, tomatoes	796 mL
1 tbsp.	chili powder	15 mL
1 tsp.	oregano	5 mL
1 tsp.	salt	5 mL

Bring water to a boil. Add lentils, cover and simmer for 30 minutes, or until lentils are tender. Drain. Brown meat and onions in a frying pan. Add tomatoes, lentils and seasonings. Bring to a boil. Reduce heat and simmer, covered, for 1 hour, stirring occasionally. **Serves:** 6.

Bran Muffins

1 cup	All-Bran cereal	250 mL
1 cup	boiling water	250 mL
½ cup	butter, softened	125 mL
1½ cups	sugar	375 mL
2	eggs, beaten	2
2½ cups	flour	625 mL
2¼ tsp.	baking soda	11 mL
1¼ tsp.	salt	6 mL
1 cup	natural bran	250 mL
2 cups	buttermilk	500 mL
1 cup	cooked dates	250 mL

Place All-Bran in a bowl and pour boiling water over it. Set aside to cool. Cream butter. Add sugar gradually beating until fluffy, then add eggs. Combine flour, baking soda, salt and bran, mixing well. Add to the butter mixture alternately with buttermilk. Add cooked dates and softened cereal, blending lightly. Fill greased muffin tins ⅔ full. Bake at 400°F (200°C) for 20-25 minutes. Let cool slightly in tins before removing.

Gruffins

¾ cup	all-purpose flour	175 mL
¾ cup	whole-wheat flour	175 mL
½ tsp.	salt	2 mL
4 tsp.	baking powder	20 mL
1 cup	granola mix	250 mL
½ cup	brown sugar	125 mL
2	eggs, beaten	2
1 cup	milk	250 mL
⅓ cup	vegetable oil	75 mL

In a large bowl, combine flours, salt and baking powder. Add granola and brown sugar, mixing well. In a small bowl, combine eggs, milk and oil. Add liquids all at once to dry ingredients. Stir until moistened — batter will be lumpy. Fill greased muffin tins ⅔ full. Bake at 425°F (220°C) for 15-20 minutes.

Corn Bread

2	eggs	2
½ cup	sugar	125 mL
1¼ cups	cream	300 mL
1 cup	cornmeal	250 mL
1 cup	all-purpose flour	250 mL
1 tbsp.	baking powder	15 mL
¼ tsp.	salt	1 mL

Beat eggs, then beat in remaining ingredients in order listed. Pour batter into a hot, buttered, 8 x 11" (3 L) baking dish. Bake at 350°F (180°C) for 20 minutes. Cut into squares. **Serving Suggestion:** Serve hot with butter and syrup. **Serves:** 8.

Molasses Brown Bread

¼ cup	shortening	50 mL
½ cup	sugar	125 mL
2	eggs	2
1 cup	applesauce	250 mL
¼ cup	light molasses	50 mL
1¼ cups	all-purpose flour	300 mL
1 cup	whole-wheat flour	250 mL
2 tsp.	baking powder	10 mL
1 tsp.	baking soda	5 mL
½ tsp.	salt	2 mL

Cream together shortening and sugar. Beat in eggs. Add applesauce and molasses, mixing well. In a separate bowl, combine flours, baking powder, baking soda and salt. Add to creamed mixture, mixing well. Pour batter into a well-greased loaf pan and bake at 350°F (180°C) for 50-55 minutes. Cool in pan for 10 minutes. Remove and cool on a rack. **Yield:** 1 loaf.

Whole-Wheat and Honey Pancakes

2 cups	whole-wheat flour	500 mL
1¼ tsp.	baking soda	6 mL
½ tsp.	salt	2 mL
2	eggs	2
2 tbsp.	honey	25 mL
2½ cups	buttermilk	625 mL
2 tbsp.	vegetable oil	25 mL

In a large bowl, combine flour, baking soda and salt. In a separate bowl, beat eggs until light. Add honey, buttermilk and oil. Add liquid ingredients to dry ingredients, stirring until just smooth. Pour approximately ¼ cup (50 mL) batter per pancake on a hot, lightly greased griddle and cook until top is bubbly and underside is golden brown. Turn and cook other side. **Serving Suggestion:** Serve with butter and honey. **Yield:** 24, 4½" (12 cm) pancakes. See photograph on page 136A.

Cracked-Wheat Bread

2 tbsp.	active dry yeast (2 pkgs.)	25 mL
½ cup	warm water	125 mL
⅔ cup	honey	150 mL
¼ cup	shortening	50 mL
1 tbsp.	salt	15 mL
3 cups	whole-wheat flour	750 mL
1¾ cups	warm water	425 mL
2½-3 cups	flour	625-750 mL
½ cup	cracked wheat	125 mL

In a blender, mix yeast and ½ cup (125 mL) warm water and let stand for 15 minutes. Add honey and shortening and blend for 15 seconds. Add salt, whole-wheat flour and water. Blend for 15 seconds. In a large bowl, combine flour and cracked wheat. Add mixture from blender, mixing well to form dough. Turn out on a lightly floured board and knead. Place in a greased bowl, cover and let rise in a warm place until doubled in bulk. Punch down dough and divide. Place in 2 greased loaf pans or 4, 1-lb. (500 g) greased coffee cans. Cover and let rise again. Bake at 375°F (190°C) for 30-40 minutes. **Yield:** 2 loaves or 4 coffee can loaves.

Cracked-Wheat Buns

2 cups	cracked wheat	500 mL
5 cups	hot water	1.25 L
2 cups	milk, scalded	500 mL
2 cups	warm water	500 mL
2 tbsp.	active dry yeast (2 pkgs.)	25 mL
1 cup	sugar	250 mL
1 cup	shortening	250 mL
2 tbsp.	salt	25 mL
5	eggs	5
13-14 cups	flour	3.25-3.5 L
	sesame seeds	

Soak cracked wheat in hot water, then cool to lukewarm. Drain. Cool scalded milk also. Then combine milk and wheat. Dissolve yeast in warm water and let foam. Add to wheat mixture. Add sugar, shortening and salt, stirring to mix. Add 4 eggs plus 1 egg yolk, reserving 1 egg white. Stir in flour and knead on a lightly floured board to form a smooth dough. Let rise in warm place until doubled in bulk. Punch down and form into buns. Place in greased baking pans and let rise again. Glaze with reserved egg white and water. Sprinkle with sesame seeds. Bake at 375°F (190°C) for 15-20 minutes.

Glazed Whole-Wheat Buns

1 tbsp.	yeast (1 pkg.)	15 mL
1 cup	milk, scalded and cooled to lukewarm	250 mL
3 tbsp.	honey	50 mL
4 tbsp.	vegetable oil	60 mL
1	egg yolk	1
1 tsp.	salt	5 mL
2½ cups	whole-wheat flour	625 mL
1 tsp.	cinnamon	5 mL
½ cup	raisins, soaked, drained and dusted with flour	125 mL
¼ cup	sunflower seeds (optional) diluted molasses OR honey	50 mL

Soften yeast in milk. Add honey, oil, egg yolk and salt. Combine flour and cinnamon and stir into first mixture. Turn into oiled bowl. Cover. Let rise in a warm place until double in bulk. Knead, adding raisins and sunflower seeds. Shape into small balls and place close together in a shallow, greased baking pan. Set in a warm place to rise again. Bake at 400°F (200°C) for about 30 minutes. Brush with molasses or honey and return to oven briefly to glaze. **Yield:** 24 small buns.

Whole-Wheat French Bread

2 tbsp.	active dry yeast (2 pkgs.)	25 mL
3½ cups	warm water	875 mL
2 tbsp.	sugar	25 mL
2 tbsp.	vegetable oil	25 mL
3 tsp.	salt	15 mL
2½ cups	whole-wheat flour	625 mL
4½ cups	all-purpose flour	1.125 L
	cornmeal	
1	egg, beaten	1
	sesame seeds	

Sprinkle yeast over warm water in a large bowl, stirring to dissolve. Let stand for 10 minutes or until foamy. Add sugar, oil, salt, whole-wheat flour and 2 cups (500 mL) all-purpose flour. Beat until smooth, gradually adding remainder of all-purpose flour to make a soft dough. Turn out onto a lightly floured board and knead until smooth and elastic, using only enough flour to keep dough from sticking. Place in a greased bowl, cover and let rise in a warm place until doubled in bulk, about 45-60 minutes. Punch down dough and divide in half. Roll each piece up tightly, jelly-roll fashion. Place each dough roll on greased baking sheets which have been sprinkled with cornmeal. Cover and let rise again, about 45 minutes. With a sharp knife, make several evenly spaced diagonal cuts ¼" (1 cm) deep in the top of each loaf. Brush with beaten egg and sprinkle with sesame seeds. Bake at 400°F (200°C) for 25 minutes. Brush quickly with cold water and bake 10 minutes longer. **Yield:** 2 loaves.

Alberta

The Best of Beef

Alberta is one of Canada's richest provinces — rich in history, in a variety of climactic features, in natural resources, in good farming land and in its people, who have come from many lands, bringing their cultures and traditions with them.

Natural resources such as coal, oil, gas, lumber and fresh-water fish have become synonymous with Alberta.

Alberta beef, pork, bacon, eggs, poultry, cheese and honey are some of the agricultural products for which Alberta is reknown.

Wheat, canola and feed grains grown on Alberta soil find their way to foreign markets as well as to other parts of Canada.

Early explorers passed through looking for the North-West Passage and in so doing they helped build up the early fur trade. Their experiences, as told to others, helped bring more people to the West.

Alberta was the province to which the first Royal North-West Mounted Police Force was sent, to stamp out the whiskey runners from the U.S.A. who were inciting trouble among the Indians and the Whites. They came first to Fort Walsh and Fort McLeod.

From the farming lands the adventurous travel west to the Rocky Mountains where the beauty is breathtaking and the rivers run east, north-east and south-east. Dams have been built on them to supply hydro power for irrigating the southern, more arid, areas.

Alberta is a very self-sufficient province where even the choosiest might find a way of life to suit them.

Best-Ever Vegetable Beef Soup, page 154

Microwave Tender Pot Roast

2½-3 lbs.	beef pot roast	1.25-1.5 kg
1 tsp.	salt	5 mL
2	large onions, sliced	2
6	peppercorns	6
1 tsp.	thyme	5 mL
½ cup	hot water OR consommé OR red wine	125 mL
4	medium carrots, sliced ¼" (1 cm) thick	4
6	small potatoes, peeled	6
2	celery stalks, cut in 1" (2.5 cm) pieces	2
	flour	

Trim excess fat from roast. Cut fat into small pieces and measure 2 tbsp. (25 mL) into a large frying pan, heating until brown. Sear roast on all sides over medium heat, until browned. Sprinkle with salt. Place roast in a 10 x 6" (2 L) microwavable baking dish. Lay onion slices on top and place peppercorns around roast. Cover with waxed paper. Cook on MEDIUM (50% power) for 20 minutes. Turn roast over. Pour hot liquid of your choice over roast. Cover and cook another 20 minutes. Remove roast from oven, reserving juices in baking dish. Check temperature of roast with meat thermometer — it should read 170°F (80°C). Wrap roast in foil and set aside for 20 minutes. Add vegetables to baking juices and cook, covered, for 15 minutes, stirring vegetables and turning potatoes once. Check meat for tenderness. Remove vegetables and add flour to remaining juices to make gravy. **Serves:** 4-6.

Best-Ever Vegetable Beef Soup

1 lb.	ground beef	500 g
2 cups	chopped onions	500 mL
1 cup	chopped celery	250 mL
1 cup	thinly sliced carrots	250 mL
6 cups	water	1.5 L
3 tbsp.	beef bouillon powder	50 mL
28 oz.	can, tomatoes, undrained, chopped	796 mL
7½ oz.	can, tomato sauce	213 mL
½ cup	pasta stars OR alphabets	125 mL
2	bay leaves	2
2 tsp.	chili powder	10 mL
2 tsp.	basil	10 mL
1 tsp.	salt	5 mL
dash	pepper	dash
2 x 14 oz.	cans, green beans, drained	2 x 398 mL

Brown ground beef in a large heavy saucepan. Drain off excess fat. Add onion, celery and carrot. Cook, stirring for 5 minutes. Add all remaining ingredients, except green beans. Bring to a boil, then reduce heat, cover and simmer for 50 minutes. Add green beans and cook until beans are heated through and pasta and vegetables are tender. Remove and discard bay leaves.
Serves: 6-8. See photograph on page 152A.

Roast Beef Salad

1-2 cups	cold, rare roast beef	250-500 mL
2	medium apples, diced	2
2	celery stalks, diced	2
4	green onions, chopped	4
4 tbsp.	minced parsley	60 mL
1	garlic clove, minced (optional)	1
6 tbsp.	vegetable oil	90 mL
3 tbsp.	wine OR cider vinegar	50 mL
	sugar to taste	
	salt and pepper to taste	

Trim excess fat from beef and cut into slivers. Toss in salad bowl with remaining ingredients. Cover and refrigerate. **Serves:** 4-6. See photograph on back cover.

Marinated Beef Kabobs

½ cup	vegetable oil	125 mL
2 tbsp.	cider vinegar	25 mL
1 tsp.	celery seed	5 mL
1 tsp.	onion salt	5 mL
¾ tsp.	garlic salt	3 mL
¾ tsp.	oregano	3 mL
½ tsp.	salt	2 mL
½ tsp.	ground black pepper	2 mL
2 lbs.	boneless shoulder OR top round of beef	1 kg
6	medium-size mushroom caps	6
2	zucchini, ½" (1 cm) slices	2

Combine first 8 ingredients in a small saucepan. Bring to a boil. Remove and cool. Cut meat into 1½" (3.5 cm) cubes. Place meat in a bowl along with mushrooms and zucchini. Add marinade and mix lightly. Cover and refrigerate for 4-6 hours, stirring occasionally. Alternate meat and vegetables on skewers. Broil on rack over hot coals or under a preheated, hot broiler for 10-15 minutes, turn and baste frequently with marinade. **Serves:** 6.

Barbecued Alberta Beef Chili Slices

1½ lbs.	round steak, in thin strips	750 g

Marinade:

½ cup	chopped onion	125 mL
2	garlic cloves, minced	2
¼ cup	vegetable oil	50 mL
3 tbsp.	vinegar	50 mL
3 tbsp.	Worcestershire sauce	50 mL
1 tbsp.	chili powder	15 mL

Sauce:

2 x 7½ oz.	cans, tomato sauce	2 x 213 mL
¼ cup	firmly packed brown sugar	50 mL
1 tsp.	dry mustard	5 mL
2 tbsp.	lemon juice	25 mL

Prepare meat and set aside. Combine all marinade ingredients, mixing well. Pour over beef and refrigerate for several hours or overnight. Remove beef, reserving marinade. In a saucepan, combine all sauce ingredients. Add reserved marinade. Bring to a boil, then reduce heat and simmer for 10 minutes. Broil or barbecue beef for desired degree of doneness, then place in a frying pan or baking dish. Pour sauce over beef. Simmer or bake, in a 350°F (180°C) oven, for 30 minutes. **Serves:** 4-6.

Stir-Fried Gingered Beef

1 lb.	flank steak	500 g
⅓ cup	water	75 mL
¼ cup	sherry	50 mL
2 tbsp.	soy sauce	25 mL
2 tbsp.	peanut oil	25 mL
1	garlic clove, minced	1
1 tsp.	shredded ginger root	5 mL
3 cups	sliced radishes	750 mL
1 cup	diagonally sliced green onions	250 mL
10 oz.	can, golden mushroom soup	284 mL
	hot, cooked rice	

Stir-Fried Gingered Beef (Cont'd.)

Slice steak in thin diagonal slices. Combine water, sherry and soy sauce. Add steak and marinate for 1 hour. Heat oil in a wok or frying pan. Add steak, marinade, garlic and ginger. Cook about 5 minutes, stirring constantly. Push mixture away from heat. Add radishes, green onions and soup. Cook 3 minutes, stirring constantly. Mix well. Serve over hot, cooked rice. **Serves:** 4.

Sweet and Sour Beef

½ cup	flour	125 mL
1 tsp.	salt	5 mL
dash	pepper	dash
2 lbs.	stewing beef, cut in bite-size pieces	1 kg
½ cup	vegetable oil	125 mL
¾ cup	water	175 mL
½ cup	brown sugar	125 mL
½ cup	vinegar	125 mL
½ cup	ketchup	125 mL
1 tbsp.	Worcestershire sauce	15 mL
1 tsp.	salt	5 mL
1	large onion, chopped	1
5-6	medium carrots, cut in ½" (1 cm) slices	5-6

Combine flour, salt and pepper and coat meat with this mixture. Brown floured meat in vegetable oil in a frying pan. Combine water, brown sugar, vinegar, ketchup, Worcestershire sauce and salt, mixing well. Stir into meat. Add onion. Cover and cook over low heat for 45 minutes, stirring occasionally. Add carrots and cook another 45 minutes on low heat until carrots and meat are tender. **Serving Suggestion:** Serve with rice or pasta. **Serves:** 8.

Murray's Pepper Steak

1½ lbs.	boneless beef steak	750 g
	salt to taste	
2	medium onions, chopped	2
10 oz.	can, beef broth	284 mL
3 tbsp.	soy sauce	50 mL
	garlic powder to taste	
1	large green pepper, cut in 1" (2.5 cm) pieces	1
2 cups	fresh OR frozen green pea pods	500 mL
1 cup	mushrooms, sliced	250 mL
2	tomatoes, chopped OR 14 oz. (398 mL) canned tomatoes	2
2 tbsp.	cornstarch	25 mL
¼ cup	cold water	50 mL

Cut steak in bite-size pieces. Brown thoroughly in a frying pan or wok and sprinkle with salt to taste. Push meat to one side and add onions. Cook, stirring, until tender but not brown. Stir in broth, soy sauce and garlic powder. Simmer for 15 minutes. Add pepper pieces, pea pods and mushrooms. Cover and simmer another 5 minutes. Add tomatoes and heat through. Blend cornstarch and water together and add to mixture. Cook, stirring, until thickened. **Serves:** 4.

Sharon's Beef Stew

2 lbs.	stewing beef OR cubed blade steak	1 kg
10 oz.	can, tomato soup	284 mL
10 oz.	can, cream of mushroom soup	284 mL
10 oz.	can, mushrooms and liquid	284 mL
1½ oz.	pkg., onion soup mix	40 g
½ cup	apple juice OR dry sherry	125 mL
	fresh vegetables prepared for stew (optional)	

Sharon's Beef Stew (Cont'd.)

Combine all ingredients, except vegetables, in a baking dish. Bake at 325°F (160°C) for 3 hours, covered, and for 1 hour, uncovered. If using vegetables, add them for the last cooking hour. **Note:** If meat seems to be drying out, add water or vegetable liquid during cooking. **Serves:** 8-10.

Low-Calorie Beef Stroganoff

1 lb.	chuck steak, cubed OR cut in 2" (5 cm) strips	500 g
2 tbsp.	flour	25 mL
½ tsp.	salt	2 mL
1 tbsp.	butter	15 mL
3	medium onions, sliced	3
3 cups	mushrooms, sliced	750 mL
1¾ cup	meat stock OR bouillon	425 mL
½ cup	tomato juice	125 mL
¼ tsp.	oregano OR basil	1 mL
¼ tsp.	dry mustard	1 mL
	salt and pepper to taste	
1 cup	plain yogurt	250 mL

Prepare meat. Combine flour and salt and dredge meat in it. Heat butter and brown meat. Add onions and mushrooms and cook until tender. Add stock, juice, oregano and mustard and bring to a boil. Reduce heat, cover and simmer until tender, about 1½ hours. Add salt and pepper. Blend in yogurt. Heat, but do NOT boil. **Serving Suggestion:** Garnish with parsley, chopped green onion, green pepper rings or tomato slices and serve in a ring of rice or over buttered noodles. **Serves: 5-6.**

Beef Croquettes

½ cup	vegetable oil	125 mL
1	medium onion, finely chopped	1
3 tbsp.	flour	50 mL
1 cup	beef broth	250 mL
2 cups	finely chopped, cooked beef	500 mL
½ tsp.	salt	2 mL
¼ tsp.	pepper	1 mL
½ tsp.	dried crushed thyme	2 mL
1 tbsp.	Worcestershire sauce	15 mL
1	egg, slightly beaten	1
¾ cup	fine, dry bread crumbs	175 mL

Heat half the oil in a heavy skillet over moderate heat. Add onion and cook, covered, until soft, about 5 minutes. Stir in flour. Cook for 1 minute, then gradually stir in beef broth. Cook, stirring, for about 1 minute or until smooth and thickened. Mix in beef, salt, pepper, thyme and Worcestershire sauce. Spread this mixture evenly in a greased 8 x 8" (2 L) baking dish. Chill in freezer for 5 minutes or until firm enough to shape. Form mixture into 4 oval patties about ¾" (2 cm) thick. Dip patties into beaten egg and coat with bread crumbs. Rinse and dry skillet. Heat remaining oil over moderate heat for 1 minute. Add the croquettes and cook until brown, 3 minutes on each side. Drain on paper towels. **Serving Suggestion:** Make croquettes ahead and refrigerate or freeze. Reheat in 350°F (180°C) oven. **Serves:** 4.

Meat Pancakes

3	eggs, separated	3
½ lb.	ground beef	250 g
¼ tsp.	baking powder	1 mL
½ tsp.	salt	2 mL
dash	pepper	dash
1 tsp.	lemon juice	5 mL
1 tbsp.	minced parsley	15 mL
1 tbsp.	grated onion	15 mL

Meat Pancakes (Cont'd.)

Lightly beat egg yolks. Add ground beef, baking powder, salt, pepper, lemon juice, parsley and onion. Mix well. Beat egg whites until stiff, then fold into meat mixture. Drop by spoonfuls onto a greased, hot griddle. When puffed and brown on the bottom, turn and brown the other side. **Serving Suggestion:** Serve at once with mushroom sauce or creamed vegetables.
Serves: 6.

Sicilian Meat Roll

2	eggs, beaten	2
½ cup	tomato juice OR water	125 mL
¾ cup	soft bread crumbs	175 mL
2 tbsp.	snipped parsley	25 mL
½ tsp.	crushed oregano	2 mL
¼ tsp.	salt	1 mL
dash	pepper	dash
1	garlic clove, minced	1
2 lbs.	ground beef	1 kg
4-6 oz.	thinly sliced cooked ham	120-170 g
6 oz.	mozzarella cheese slices	170 g

In a bowl, combine eggs and tomato juice. Stir in bread crumbs, parsley, oregano, salt, pepper, garlic and ground beef. Mix well. Place on waxed paper or foil and pat mixture into a 10" x 8" (25 x 20 cm) rectangle. Arrange ham and cheese slices on top of meat, leaving a small margin around edges. Starting from short edge, carefully roll up using waxed paper to lift. Seal edges and ends with pressure. Place seam-side-down in a 9 x 13" (4 L) baking dish. Bake at 350°F (180°C) for 1½ hours. **Note:** Center will be pink due to ham.
Serves: 8.

Meatza Pie

1 lb.	ground beef	500 g
½-1 tsp.	garlic salt	2-5 mL
½ cup	fine dry bread crumbs OR 1 cup (250 mL) soft bread crumbs	125 mL
⅔ cup	evaporated milk	150 mL
⅓ cup	ketchup OR tomato paste	75 mL
1 cup	sliced mushrooms	250 mL
2-3	cheese slices, cut into strips	2-3
¼ tsp.	oregano	1 mL
2 tsp.	grated Parmesan cheese	10 mL

Place beef, garlic salt and bread crumbs in a 9" (23 cm) pie plate. Add evaporated milk and mix with a fork. Spread evenly, raising a rim about ½" (1 cm) high around edge. Spread ketchup over meat to rim. Arrange cheese slices over top. Sprinkle with oregano and Parmesan cheese. Bake at 450°F (230°C) for 20 minutes or until cheese is melted and lightly browned. **Serves:** 6.

Saucy Short Ribs

4 lbs.	beef short ribs	2 kg
1	medium onion, sliced	1
½ cup	sliced celery	125 mL
1¼ cups	ketchup	300 mL
¼ cup	brown sugar	50 mL
¼ cup	vinegar	50 mL
¼ cup	flour	50 mL
1 tbsp.	Worcestershire sauce	15 mL
½ tsp.	salt	2 mL
¼ tsp.	dry mustard	1 mL

Arrange ribs in a baking dish, large enough to allow ribs to lay flat on bottom. Brown both sides of ribs in a 350°F (180°C) oven. When browned, arrange onion and celery on top of ribs. Continue baking for 30 minutes. Combine all remaining ingredients, mixing well. Pour over ribs. Bake until tender, about 60 minutes. **Serves:** 6-8.

World's Best Meat Loaf

2 lbs.	ground beef	1 kg
1 cup	mayonnaise	250 mL
2 tbsp.	finely chopped onion	25 mL
1½ cups	soft bread crumbs	375 mL
2 tsp.	salt	10 mL
¼ tsp.	pepper	1 mL
6-8	potatoes, cooked, mashed	6-8
2 cups	hot, sliced, cooked beets	500 mL

Combine meat, mayonnaise, onion, bread crumbs and seasonings. Turn into a 1½-quart (1.5 L) tube pan, bake at 325°F (160°C) for 75 minutes. Unmold on large platter. Fill centre with mashed potatoes, surround with beets. **Serves:** 8.

Lasagne

¾ lb.	lasagne noodles	375 g
2 tbsp.	vegetable oil	25 mL
¾ lb.	ground beef	375 g
	salt and pepper to taste	
3 cups	spaghetti sauce	750 mL
½ cup	water	125 mL
10½ oz.	pkg., frozen spinach (opt.)	300 g
2 cups	cottage cheese	500 mL
1	egg, beaten	1
6 oz.	mozzarella cheese slices	170 g

Cook lasagne noodles. Rinse in cold water and set aside. In a frying pan, heat oil and brown ground beef. Drain off excess fat and season meat with salt and pepper. Stir in spaghetti sauce and water. Bring to a boil. Reduce heat and simmer, uncovered, for 5 minutes. Cook spinach, if using, and drain well. Mix spinach with cottage cheese, beaten egg and salt and pepper. Spread a few spoonfuls of meat sauce over the bottom of a 9 x 13" (4 L) baking dish. Arrange ¼ of the lasagne noodles over the sauce and cover with ⅓ of the remaining sauce. Arrange another layer of lasagne noodles on top. Spread with ⅓ of the cottage cheese mixture. Alternate layers twice more and top with cheese slices. Bake at 350°F (180°C) for 30 minutes. Let stand before serving. **Serves:** 6-8.

Harvest Casserole

1	small head cabbage	1
½ cup	uncooked brown rice	125 mL
	boiling water	
½ lb.	side bacon, 1" (2.5 cm) cubes	250 g
1½ lbs.	ground beef	750 g
½ tsp.	hamburger seasoning	2 mL
¼ tsp.	rosemary	1 mL
¼ tsp.	onion salt	1 mL
	salt and pepper to taste	
28 oz.	can, tomatoes	796 mL

Chop cabbage coarsely and spread in bottom of large, greased baking dish. Sprinkle rice over cabbage. Add boiling water to cover to a depth of ½" (1 cm). Fry bacon in frying pan until browned but not crisp. Spread bacon over cabbage and rice. Brown ground beef in bacon drippings. Add hamburger seasoning, rosemary, onion salt, salt and pepper during cooking. Add tomatoes and simmer 5 minutes. Drain off fat. Add tomatoes and beef to cabbage and rice. Cover and bake at 350°F (180°C) for 1½ hours. **Serves:** 8-10.

Burger Corn Casserole

2 tbsp.	vegetable oil	25 mL
1½ lbs.	ground beef	750 g
1	large onion, chopped	1
1½ tsp.	salt	7 mL
½ tsp.	pepper	2 mL
14 oz.	can, cream corn	398 mL
10 oz.	can, tomato soup	284 mL
7½ oz.	can, tomato sauce	213 mL
3 cups	cooked pasta	750 mL
1 cup	grated Cheddar cheese	250 mL

Heat oil in frying pan. Add ground beef, onion, salt and pepper, cooking slowly until all pink color has disappeared from meat. Add corn, soup and sauce, stirring to mix. Stir cooked pasta into mixture. Pour into a 3-quart (3 L) baking dish. Sprinkle with grated cheese. Bake at 350°F (180°C) for 1 hour. If cheese begins to dry out, cover after half cooking time. **Serves:** 6.

Busy-Day Casserole

6	medium potatoes, peeled and sliced	6
4	carrots, peeled and sliced	4
1	onion, finely chopped	1
1 cup	uncooked long-grain rice	250 mL
2 lbs.	ground beef	1 kg
1 tsp.	salt	5 mL
dash	pepper	dash
10 oz.	can, tomato soup	284 mL
	water	

In a greased, medium-sized roaster or large baking dish, place vegetables in layers as listed. Sprinkle rice over vegetables. Form beef into patties and arrange over rice. Sprinkle with salt and pepper. Add soup and enough water to just cover vegetables and rice. Cover and bake at 325°F (160°C) for 1½-2 hours, or until vegetables are tender and rice is cooked. **Serves:** 8-10.

Beef Buns

3 tbsp.	chopped onion	50 mL
	shortening	
1 lb.	lean ground beef	500 g
1 tsp.	salt	5 mL
7½ oz.	can, tomato sauce	213 mL
2 tbsp.	ketchup	25 mL
½ tsp.	chili powder	2 mL
2 tbsp.	brown sugar	25 mL
1 tsp.	dry mustard	5 mL
2 tbsp.	lemon juice	25 mL
1 tsp.	cornstarch	5 mL
1 cup	diced celery	250 mL
10-12	buns	10-12

In a large saucepan, sauté onion in shortening. Add beef and brown, stirring occasionally. Sprinkle with salt after half the cooking time. Drain well. Blend all other ingredients, except celery and buns. Add to the meat mixture. Add diced celery. Simmer for 10 minutes. Serve on a bun. **Yield:** 10-12.

Chinese Meat Balls

1½ lbs.	ground beef	750 g
½ cup	chopped onion	125 mL
10 oz.	mushrooms, drained and finely chopped	284 mL
1 tsp.	salt	5 mL
dash	pepper	dash
3 tbsp.	soy sauce	50 mL
1	egg, beaten	1
2 tbsp.	cornstarch	25 mL
1 cup	sliced carrots	250 mL
2	medium green peppers, sliced	2
14 oz.	can, pineapple chunks, reserve juice for sauce	398 mL

Sauce:

2 tbsp.	sugar	25 mL
1 tbsp.	soy sauce	15 mL
¼ tsp.	salt	1 mL
dash	pepper	dash
2 tbsp.	vinegar	25 mL
1 tbsp.	cornstarch	15 mL
	water	

Combine beef, onion, mushrooms, salt, pepper, soy sauce, egg and cornstarch, mixing well. Form into 1" (2.5 cm) balls. Brown in frying pan, then drain off excess fat. Add carrots, peppers and pineapple chunks to meatballs and put in covered baking dish. Bake at 375°F (190°C) for 30 minutes. Prepare sauce by combining reserved pineapple juice, sugar, soy sauce, salt, pepper and vinegar in a saucepan. Bring to a boil. Dissolve cornstarch in a small amount of water and add to sauce. Cook, stirring, until thickened. Pour over meatballs.
Serving Suggestion: Serve over pasta or rice. **Serves:** 8-10.

British Columbia

Wild Cooking

The history of our western-most province and the fishing industry go hand and hand. The fishing grounds of British Columbia were coveted by many nations and many political battles have been fought over the famous Fraser River Salmon. Today, many years later, technological developments in processing and storage allow Canadians from coast to coast to enjoy the abundant harvest of these fisheries.

The W. I. cooks of British Columbia have chosen to spotlight two of their favorite fish in their traditional recipes. The salmon is one of the most famous products of B. C. For a real summer cooking experience, try the recipe for Barbecued Salmon. This method is very similar to that historically used by the Native people. They used green sticks to enclose the salmon, instead of the wire used today.

A lesser known, but equally delicious fish, is the Eulachons or "candlefish". Eulachons is a sea-fish of the salmon family found only on the Northwest coast of North America. It is about the size of a smelt. The name "candlefish" was derived from the fact that by passing a wick through the whole fish, it could be used as a candle. Eulachons leave the sea for a few weeks each year to travel up the Fraser and Skeena rivers where they are so plentiful they can be scooped out of the water by hand. These small fish are traditionally either pan-fried or smoked.

British Columbia provides a unique and varied collection of recipes featuring wild berries, fish and game. Here is a tip for those game recipes — a piece of apple, onion, carrot or celery placed inside the body cavity will absorb and reduce the gamey flavor. Discard the apple or vegetable after cooking. So, get ready for some "wild cooking", compliments of British Columbia!

Barbecued Salmon, page 169

Barbecued Salmon

6-10 lbs.	fresh salmon, boned, with skin intact, in 1 piece	3-5 kg
½ cup	vegetable oil	125 mL
2 tbsp.	lemon juice	25 mL
½ tsp.	rosemary leaves	2 mL
	salt and pepper to taste	

Prepare salmon. Combine oil, lemon juice and rosemary and let stand at least 1 hour. Strain. Lay the salmon open over half of a fine mesh chicken wire square, measuring 30" (90 cm) square. Fold other half of wire over fish, securing with 2-3" (5-7.5 cm) nails twisted through wire. Brush skin side of fish liberally with oil mixture. Sprinkle with salt and pepper. Broil, open-side-down, approximately 3" (7.5 cm) from hot coals. Cook until salmon flakes easily with a fork, about 10 minutes. To broil, place fish, skin-side-down, on greased aluminum foil on a broiler rack. Brush with oil mixture and season. Broil 3" (7.5 cm) from heat source until fish flakes easily with a fork, about 20 minutes. **Serves:** 8-12. See photograph on page 168A.

Eulachons

fresh eulachons	
beaten egg	
bread crumbs	

Clean and dry eulachons. Dip in beaten egg and roll in bread crumbs. Place on a buttered baking sheet in a hot oven. Cook until crisp and brown.

High Bush Cranberry Jelly

cranberry juice
water
sugar

Boil cranberries, in a small amount of water, until soft. Put through a collander, then place in a jelly bag to drain. Reserve cranberry pulp for making Cranberry Ketchup. Measure drained juice. Add equal amounts of sugar. Bring to boiling point and simmer gently until jelly stage is reached (mixture will sheet). Pour into hot sterile jars and seal.

High Bush Cranberry Ketchup

3 qts.	prepared cranberry pulp	3L
1 tsp.	ground cloves	5 mL
1 tsp.	cinnamon	5 mL
½ tsp.	ground ginger	2 mL
¼ tsp.	red pepper flakes	1 mL
8	medium onions, chopped	8
1 qt.	vinegar	1 L
2 lbs.	brown sugar	1 kg

Prepare berries by boiling them in a small amount of water until soft. Put through collander, then place in a jelly bag to drain. Reserve drained juice for making jelly. Measure 3-quarts (3 L) of pulp and add remaining ingredients. Boil until thickened, about 1 hour, stirring occasionally to prevent burning.

Chokecherry Wine

4 qts.	chokecherries	4 L
5 qts.	boiling water	5 L
6 cups	sugar	1.5 L
1	orange, sliced	1
1	lemon, sliced	1
1 tbsp.	active dry yeast (1 pkg.)	15 mL

Place berries in a crock and pour boiling water over them. Crush berries lightly, being careful not to crush pits as they will cause a bitter taste. Let stand for 5 days, stirring daily. Strain and add sugar, fruit and yeast. Let stand another 5 days, then strain and bottle. Make in the berry season and let sit until Christmas.

Dandelion Jelly

1 qt.	dandelion blossoms*	1 L
2 qts.	water	2 L
6 cups	sugar	1.5 L
½ cup	lemon juice	125 mL
few drops	yellow food coloring	few drops
2 oz.	powdered fruit pectin (1 box)	57 g

Wash dandelion blossoms. Cover with water and simmer for 20 minutes. Strain. Measure 3½ cups (875 mL) dandelion juice. To juice, add sugar, mixing well. Add lemon juice and coloring. Place over high heat and bring to a boil, stirring constantly. At once, stir in pectin. Bring to a full rolling boil and boil hard for 1 minute, stirring constantly. Remove from heat, skim off foam with a metal spoon and pour quickly into sterilized jars. Seal. *Note: Pick dandelion blossoms in spring as later in the year they become bitter. Yield: 4 cups (1 L).

Dandelion Lunch

2 tbsp.	butter	25 mL
2 tbsp.	flour	25 mL
1½ cups	milk	375 mL
	salt and pepper to taste	
1½-2 cups	washed, chopped fresh dandelion greens	375-500 mL
4	lightly buttered toast slices	4

Melt butter. Stir in flour to make a paste. Add milk and cook, stirring until thick. Season sauce with salt and pepper. Keep warm. When ready to serve, stir dandelion greens into sauce and serve on hot toast. **Serves:** 4.

Fireweed Jelly

	fireweed blossoms*	
	boiling water	
2 oz.	powdered fruit pectin (1 box)	57 g
2½ cups	sugar	625 mL

Fill an 8-quart (8 L) preserving kettle half full with fireweed blossoms. Cover with boiling water and simmer for 1 hour, do NOT boil. Strain and measure 2¼ cups (550 mL) of juice into preserving kettle. Add pectin to juice and cook as directed on pectin package. Then add sugar and bring to a full rolling boil. Boil for 1 minute. Pour into sterilized jars and seal. ***Note:** Gather fireweed blossoms when first out, making sure plants have not been sprayed. If fireweed grows too tall, the coloring is lost and a little red coloring must be added. **Yield:** 3 cups (750 mL).

Huckleberry Cream Cheese Pie

Base:

½ cup	melted butter	125 mL
1⅓ cups	graham wafer crumbs	325 mL

Filling:

8 oz.	pkg., cream cheese, softened	250 g
2	eggs	2
½ cup	sugar	125 mL
¼ tsp.	salt	1 mL
1 tsp.	vanilla	5 mL

Topping:

2 cups	huckleberries	500 mL
½ cup	sugar	125 mL
½ cup	water	125 mL
2 tbsp.	cornstarch	25 mL

Combine base ingredients and press into a pie plate to form a crust. Prepare the filling by beating the cream cheese, eggs, sugar, salt and vanilla together until creamy and smooth. Pour into prepared pie plate and bake at 325°F (160°C) for 25-30 minutes or just until filling sets. Cool. Combine topping ingredients in a saucepan and cook until thick. Cool. Spread cooled topping over cooled pie. **Serves:** 6.

Preserved Saskatoons

Saskatoon berries, washed and sorted
rhubarb, sliced
water
sugar

Fill canning jars half-full with Saskatoon berries. Fill to neck with sliced rhubarb. Make a medium syrup using 3 cups (750 mL) of sugar to every 4 cups (1 L) of water. Stir well before heating. Bring slowly to a boil, cook only until the sugar dissolves. Keep hot until needed. Pour syrup over fruit, leaving ½" (1 cm) head space. Adjust lids and process in boiling water bath for 20 minutes. **Note:** Amounts of ingredients may be varied to suit need.

Rose Hip Butter

3 cups	rose hips	750 mL
1	lemon, grated peel of	1
1 cup	cold water	250 mL
¼ cup	lemon juice	50 mL
3 cups	sugar	750 mL
¼ tsp.	ground ginger	1 mL
½ tsp.	ground cardamom	2 mL
1 tbsp.	butter	15 mL

Remove stems and blossom ends from rose hips. Place in a saucepan along with lemon peel and water. Boil until fruit is tender. Empty into blender and add lemon juice. Reduce to purée. Pour into a large saucepan and add sugar, ginger, cardamom and butter. Cook, stirring frequently, until thick. Test as for jam. Pour into sterilized jars and seal. **Yield:** 4 cups (1 L).

Drying Mushrooms

Gather only young, well-known species. Wash, if necessary. As a precaution to prevent spoilage, boil mushrooms in water for 3 minutes. To dry, thread mushrooms on a string or lay them out on paper towels or on a screen. Keep them in a warm, dry, clean place, free from moisture. When well dried, keep mushrooms in sealed, sterilized jars. To reconstitute, soak dried mushrooms in warm water for several hours and use in stews, gravies, sauces or soups.

Piquant Dill Trout

1 lb.	lake trout, cleaned	500 g
	salted flour	
1 tbsp.	vegetable oil	15 mL
2 tbsp.	chopped onion	25 mL
½ tsp.	dry mustard	2 mL
1 tsp.	parsley flakes	5 mL
¼ cup	chopped dill pickles	50 mL
1 tbsp.	lemon juice	15 mL
2 tbsp.	chili sauce	25 mL
½ cup	sour cream	125 mL
¼ tsp.	sweet basil	1 mL

Cut trout into 4 serving-size pieces and sprinkle lightly with salted flour. Arrange, skin-side-down, in a greased baking dish. In a frying pan, heat oil and sauté onions until tender and transparent, about 3-4 minutes. Add remaining ingredients and mix with onions. Spread mixture over fish. Bake at 400°F (200°C) for 15-25 minutes or until fish flakes easily with a fork. **Serves:** 4.

Smoked Fillet of Trout

whole trout
salt
dark brown sugar
hickory, rotten spruce OR
green alder wood, for
smoking
soy sauce (optional)

Fillet both sides of trout and lay in a large pan, skin-side-down. Add salt and sugar to each layer, rubbing it in with your hands. Use same amount of salt as you would for frying. Layer until pan is full or you run out of fish. Let stand overnight. Lay fillets on smoke house wire racks, skin-side-down. Do not hang. Smoke for about 24 hours with cook smoke from hickory, rotten spruce or green alder wood. A touch of soy sauce may be used. Fish should be done when it peels off dry when fillets are bent. A hard shiny glaze should be apparent on the surface of the fish and it should flake easily with a fork. To store, put in onion bag and hang in cool, dry place. Do not freeze.

Roast Wild Duck

3-5 lbs.	wild duck	1.5-2 kg
	salt and pepper to taste	
1	medium apple, sliced	1
1	small onion, sliced	1
	wine OR orange juice	

Season duck, inside and out, with salt and pepper. Put apple and onion slices into cavity of duck. Place on rack of roasting pan. Do not cover. (If it is an older bird, cover for last half of cooking time.) Bake at 325°F (160°C) for 2-3 hours or until tender. Baste occasionally during cooking with wine or juice. Remove apple and onion before serving and discard. **Serves:** 6.

Special Grouse

2 OR 3	breasts of grouse, well cleaned	2 OR 3
	butter OR bacon fat	
1	medium onion, diced	1
½	garlic clove, minced	½
½ cup	white wine	125 mL

Sauté breasts in butter or bacon fat, then place in baking dish. Sauté onion and garlic. Add wine. Pour over grouse. Cover and bake at 350°F (180°C) for 45 minutes or until tender. **Serves:** 2-4.

Baked Wild Rabbit

1	rabbit, cleaned and washed	1
1	egg, beaten	1
	salt and pepper to taste	
	bread crumbs	
1	onion, sliced	1
1 cup	sweet cream	250 mL

Cut rabbit in pieces. Dip in beaten egg. Season with salt and pepper and roll in bread crumbs. Layer in baking dish. Add onion slices. Pour cream over top. Bake at 350°F (180°C) for 1¼ hours until tender. **Serves:** 4.

Deer or Elk Soup

1	large deer or elk bone with meat	1
	water	
3	large carrots, diced	3
1 cup	diced turnips	250 mL
4	medium potatoes, diced	4
1	small onion, diced	1
½ cup	uncooked rice	125 mL
4 cups	tomatoes	1 L
	salt and pepper to taste	

Cover bone and meat with water. Boil for 4 hours. Remove bone and reserve liquid. Remove meat from bone, cut into chunks and return to liquid. Add vegetables, rice, tomatoes and seasonings and bring to a boil. Reduce heat and simmer until vegetables are tender, about 1 hour. **Serves:** 8.

Barbecued Venison Spareribs

2 lbs.	venison spareribs	1 kg
½ cup	flour	125 mL
	salt and pepper to taste	
	butter	
1	medium onion, chopped	1
½ cup	water	125 mL
2 tbsp.	Worcestershire sauce	25 mL
½ cup	lemon juice	125 mL
½ tsp.	salt	2 mL
2 tbsp.	brown sugar	25 mL
1 cup	ketchup OR chili sauce	250 mL
½ tsp.	paprika	2 mL

Dredge spareribs in flour seasoned with salt and pepper. Heat butter in a Dutch oven and brown ribs until tender. In a frying pan, sauté chopped onion until transparent. In a saucepan, combine remaining ingredients. Heat and simmer for 20 minutes. Add onions to sauce, then pour sauce over spareribs. Bake at 350°F (180°C) for about 1 hour. **Serves:** 6.

Grandma Schultz's Moose Meat Sausage

9 lbs.	ground moose meat	4.5 kg
3 lbs.	ground pork	1.5 kg
1 cup	flour	250 mL
4 tbsp.	pepper	60 mL
2 tbsp.	mustard seed	25 mL
6 tbsp.	coarse salt	90 mL
4 tbsp.	sage	60 mL
1 tbsp.	crushed garlic	15 mL
1½ tbsp.	sugar	22 mL
2 tbsp.	red barbecue salt	25 mL
1½ cups	boiling water	375 mL

Mix all ingredients well. Put into sausage skins, tying well in desired lengths. Smoke sausage in smokehouse, or use barbecue. To use barbecue, make a small fire on a foil pie plate using dry poplar or willow. When half burned down, smother with oats. Lift barbecue rack as high as possible and place sausages on top. Cover with an old blanket to keep smoke in, but leave front open. Smoke for 1½ hours. Fire may have to be made several times, always on a plate away from the sausages, as they must not get hot. After smoking time, sausages should be fairly firm. Plunge them into a large kettle of rapidly boiling water and return to a boil for 10-15 minutes. Remove and dry sausages on rack. To prepare sausages for eating, bake at 350°F (180°C) for 15-20 minutes. Sausages may be frozen. To reheat, double baking time.

Roast Caribou

6	onions	6
	melted butter	
1	bay leaf	1
5 lbs.	caribou roast	2.5 kg
	salt and pepper to taste	
	juniper berries	
	buttermilk	
	High Bush Cranberry Jelly (see recipe, page 170).	

Roast Caribou (Cont'd.)

Chop 3 onions finely. Add to melted butter along with bay leaf. Soak roast in butter mixture, refrigerated, for 3-5 days, turning daily. Remove roast and pat dry with paper towels. Season with salt, pepper and juniper berries. Place in a baking dish. Place remaining 3 onions around roast. Baste with buttermilk. Bake at 400°F (200°C) for about 2 hours; 25 minutes per pound (500 g). Glaze with cranberry jelly. Gravy can be made using buttermilk or sour cream. **Serves:** 8-10.

Moose Meat Short Ribs

	moose short ribs	
	flour	
	salt, pepper, allspice, marjoram, chili powder, garlic, parsley, thyme and dry mustard to taste	
	bacon fat	
1	bay leaf	1
½ cup	wine	125 mL
3 tbsp.	tomato paste	50 mL
1 cup	chopped celery	250 mL
1	onion, chopped	1
2	carrots, finely diced	2
10 oz.	can, mushrooms, drained	284 mL

Cut ribs into 3" (7.5 cm) pieces. Season flour with the spices to taste. Place seasoned flour and ribs in a bag and shake to coat. Brown ribs in hot bacon fat. Add bay leaf. Add wine and tomato paste. Cook very slowly until tender. During last ½ hour of cooking, add celery, onion, carrots and mushrooms. Discard bay leaf before serving. **Serving Suggestion:** Serve on fluffy rice.

Index